Beginning
Vue 3
Development

Greg Lim

Table of Contents

PREFACE

About this book

In this book, we take you on a fun, hands-on and pragmatic journey to quickly learn Vue and get familiar with how it works. You'll start building Vue apps within minutes. Every section is written in a bite-sized manner and straight to the point as we don't want to waste your time (and most certainly ours) on the content you don't need. In the end, you will have what it takes to develop a real-life app.

Requirements

Basic familiarity with HTML, CSS, JavaScript and object-oriented programming. No prior knowledge of Vue is required as we start from basics.

Contact and Code Examples

The source codes used in this book can be obtained by emailing support@i-ducate.com.

Send any comments or questions concerning this book to https://twitter.com/greglim81 or email support@i-ducate.com.

Chapter 1: Introduction

What is Vue?

Vue is a frontend JavaScript framework to build dynamic user interfaces. It is similar to other frontends frameworks such as React, Angular, Svelte where you create reusable UI components to build interactive user interfaces.

Vue is generally used (but not limited) to create single page apps that run on the client. The app makes HTTP requests and responds to a backend server (eg. NodeJS, PHP, Django).

Why use Vue?

Vue was designed by Evan You and released in 2014. Evan worked with AngularJS at Google. He wanted to extract the parts he liked from AngularJS and create a new but lightweight framework.

Vue has seen a huge rise in popularity and is considered one of the main front-end frameworks. It is widely used by a range of businesses from Gitlab to Alibaba. It has been adopted by the PHP framework Laravel as its default library to build client-side apps.

Vue is also easier to learn than other frameworks like React. Most of the things that are complicated with other frameworks are simple with Vue. You can do a lot more with less code.

Vue has a great community which makes available all kinds of pre-built components and libraries to provide common functions such as client-side routing, state management and server-side rendering. Many are maintained by the official Vue team. It is easy to get help with your problems on various support sites and forums.

Step by Step

I will teach you about Vue from scratch in step by step fashion. You will build an application where you can input search terms and receive the search results via GitHub RESTful API (fig. 1).

Search
daniel
Submit
Id
Avatar
Login
URL
635
daniel
https://github.com/daniel
1390773
dkayiwa
https://github.com/dkayiwa
50654
danielmiessler
https://github.com/danielmiessler
6912596
DanielHe4rt
https://github.com/DanielHe4rt

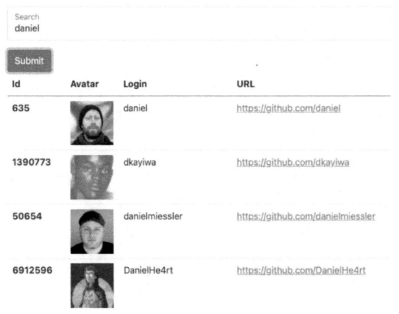

Figure 1

In the end, you will also build a real-world To-do application with full C.R.U.D. operations (fig. 2).

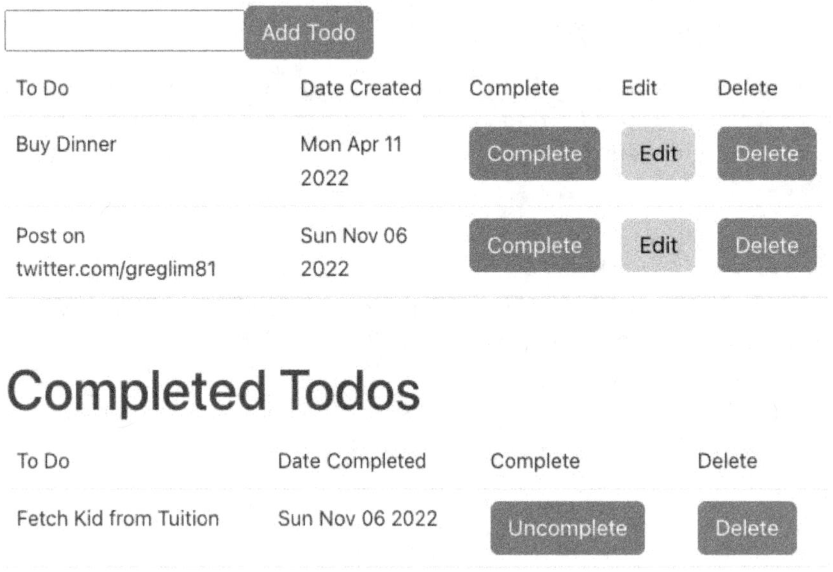

Add Todo
To Do
Date Created
Complete
Edit
Delete
Buy Dinner
Mon Apr 11 2022
Complete
Edit
Delete
Post on twitter.com/greglim81
Sun Nov 06 2022
Complete
Edit
Delete
Completed Todos
To Do
Date Completed
Complete
Delete
Fetch Kid from Tuition
Sun Nov 06 2022
Uncomplete
Delete

Figure 2

These are the patterns you see in a lot of real-world applications. In this book, you will learn how to implement these patterns with Vue.

Thinking in Components

A Vue app is made up of independent and reusable components. For example, if we want to build a storefront module like what we see on Amazon, we can divide it into three components. The search bar component, sidebar component and products component.

Components can also contain other components. For example, in *products* component where we display a list of products, we do so using multiple *product* components. Also, in each *product* component, we can have a *rating* component (fig. 3).

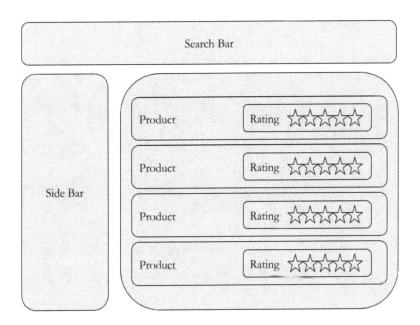

Figure 3

The benefit of such an architecture helps us to break up a large application into smaller manageable components. Plus, we can reuse components within the application or even in a different application. For example, we can re-use the rating component in a different application.

A Vue component self-contains template (HTML markup), logic (JavaScript) and styling (CSS) in a *.vue* file. A Vue component is also thus called a Single-File-Component since it encapsulates all three in a single file.

Because the logic and UI for a component are kept together, the components are easier to maintain

Below is an example of a product component that displays a simple string containing the product name:

Analyze Code

```
<template>
  <h1>The product name is {{name}}!</h1>
</template>


<script>
  export default{
    data(){
      return{
        name = 'bag';
      }
    }
  }
</script>


<style scoped>
  h1{
     color: blue;
  }
<style>
```

Code Explanation

The above illustrates the basic layout of a Vue component. There are three main separate areas: <template>, <script> and <style>.

```
<template>
  <h1>The product name is {{name}}!</h1>
</template>
```

We have the *template* section containing markup to output HTML. In the curly braces, you can put any JavaScript code, e.g. variables, expressions, conditionals, loops (as we shall see later). In the template, Vue uses declarative rendering where we can declaratively describe HTML output based on JavaScript state. For e.g., outputting HTML based on the *name* variable.

```
<script>
  export default{
    data(){
      return{
        name = 'bag';
      }
    }
  }
</script>
```

We next have the <script> section to contain the component's logic. Using JavaScript, you can set values for variables, define props, create custom/life-cycle methods etc. In the example, we declared a *name* variable which we refer in the markup: **<h1>The product name is {{name}}!</h1>**.

This outputs the HTML "The product name is bag".

```
<style scoped>
  h1{
    color: blue;
  }
<style>
```

You specify the CSS you want to apply in the <style> tag. *scoped* means the style pertains only to this component.

This is the big picture of thinking in terms of components. As you progress through this book, you will see more of this in action.

Setting Up

Installing Node

First, we need to install NodeJS. NodeJS is a server-side language and we don't need it because we are not writing any server-side code. We mostly need it because of its *npm* or Node Package Manager. *npm* is very popular for managing dependencies of your applications. We will use *npm* to install other later tools that we need.

Get the latest version of NodeJS from *nodejs.org* and install it on your machine. Installing NodeJS should be pretty easy and straightforward.

To check if Node has been properly installed, type the below on your command line (Command Prompt on Windows or Terminal on Mac):

Execute in Terminal

```
node -v
```

and you should see the node version displayed.

To see if npm is installed, type the below on your command line:

Execute in Terminal

```
npm -v
```

and you should see the npm version displayed.

Creating a Vue Application

The easiest way to start a Vue project is to run the following command in the Terminal:

Execute in Terminal

```
npm init vue@latest
```

create-vue, the official Vue project scaffolding tool will be installed and executed.

You will be asked some questions:
✔ Project name: ... <your-project-name>
✔ Add TypeScript? ... No / Yes
✔ Add JSX Support? ... No / Yes
✔ Add Vue Router for Single Page Application development? ... No / Yes
✔ Add Pinia for state management? ... No / Yes
✔ Add Vitest for Unit testing? ... No / Yes
✔ Add Cypress for both Unit and End-to-End testing? ... No / Yes
✔ Add ESLint for code quality? ... No / Yes
✔ Add Prettier for code formatting? ... No / Yes

If you are unsure about an option, just choose 'No' by hitting *enter* for now. Note that this assigns a default project name 'vue-project'.

This will create a project in a newly created <your-project-name> folder. Next, run the following:

Execute in Terminal

```
cd <your-project-name>
npm install
```

```
npm run dev
```

This creates a new project in the **<your-project-name>** directory, installs its dependencies (we look at them later) and starts a dev server on http://localhost:5173/ (fig. 4).

```
MacBook-Air:vue-project user$ npm run dev

> vue-project@0.0.0 dev
> vite


  VITE v3.0.9  ready in    ms

  →  Local:   http://127.0.0.1:5173/
     Network: use      to expose
```

Figure 4

If you point your browser to localhost:5173, you will see the Vue project running (fig. 5):

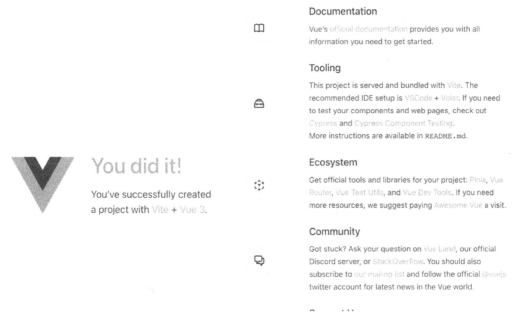

Figure 5

Project File Review

Now let's look at the project files with a code editor. In this book, we recommend using VSCode (https://code.visualstudio.com/) which is a good, lightweight and cross-platform editor from Microsoft. We also recommend installing the 'Volar' extension (fig. 6).

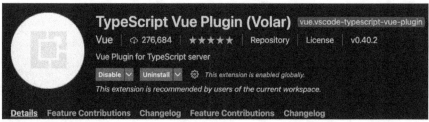

Figure 6

Volar gives you syntax highlighting, TypeScript support, and intellisense for template expressions and component props within Vue components.

When you open the project folder in VSCode editor, you will find a couple of files (fig. 7).

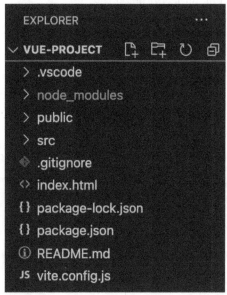

Figure 7

We will not go through all the files as our focus is to get started with our first app quickly, but we will briefly go through some of the more important files and folders.

Our app lives in the *src* folder. All components go here. Any other files outside of this folder are meant to support building your app. In the course of this book, you will come to appreciate the uses for the rest of the library files and folders.

14

In the *src* folder, we have *main.js* which is the entry point for our app where we initialize and bring in the main App component:

Analyze Code

```
import { createApp } from 'vue'
import App from './App.vue'

import './assets/main.css'

createApp(App).mount('#app')
```

A Vue application starts by creating a new application instance with the *createApp* function. We import and use the root component *App* from *./App.vue* (explained in the next section).

We call *mount()* to render App in *#app* selector of index.html (more on that later):

```
<!DOCTYPE html>
<html lang="en">
  <head>
    ...
  </head>
  <body>
    <div id="app"></div>
    <script type="module" src="/src/main.js"></script>
  </body>
</html>
```

App.vue

App component is defined in *src/App.vue*:

Analyze Code

```
<script setup>
import HelloWorld from './components/HelloWorld.vue'
import TheWelcome from './components/TheWelcome.vue'
</script>

<template>
  <header>
    <img alt="Vue logo" class="logo" src="./assets/logo.svg" … />

    <div class="wrapper">
      <HelloWorld msg="You did it!" />
    </div>
  </header>
```

```
  <main>
    <TheWelcome />
  </main>
</template>

<style scoped>
...
</style>
```

App is the root component that contains other components i.e. *HelloWorld* and *TheWelcome* as its children. Notice that it has three sections:
- *script* – contains logic
- *template* – outputs HTML
- *style* – contains CSS styles

In *script*, we import *HelloWorld* and *TheWelcome*. In *template*, we can then use it:

```
<template>
  <header>
      ...
    <div class="wrapper">
      <HelloWorld msg="You did it!" />
    </div>
  </header>

  <main>
    <TheWelcome />
  </main>
</template>
```

We discuss more on how to define and compose multiple components together later.

package.json

package.json is the node package configuration which lists the packages our project uses. For example, in *dependencies*, it uses the 'vue' framework and in *devDependencies*, it uses the 'vite' module as indicated in **bold**:

Analyze Code

```
{
  "name": "vue-project",
  "version": "0.0.0",
  "scripts": {
      ...
  },
  "dependencies": {
    "vue": "^3.2.37"
```

```
  },
  "devDependencies": {
    "@vitejs/plugin-vue": "^3.0.1",
    "vite": "^3.0.4"
  }
}
```

Under *scripts*, we have the *build* command (*npm run build*) to compile our Vue code into optimized JavaScript for production.

Analyze Code

```
...
  "scripts": {
    "dev": "vite",
    "build": "vite build",
    "preview": "vite preview --port 4173"
  },
...
```

We also have the *dev* command to start our dev server with live reload. i.e. Vue auto-detects code changes and the app reloads automatically with the revised code so you don't have to refresh the page every time your code changes.

index.html

The root folder contains index.html which is our Single Page Application loaded in the browser:

Analyze Code

```html
<!DOCTYPE html>
<html lang="en">
  <head>
    <meta charset="UTF-8" />
    <link rel="icon" href="/favicon.ico" />
    <meta name="viewport" content="width=device-width, initial-scale=1.0"
/>
    <title>Vite App</title>
  </head>
  <body>
    <div id="app"></div>
    <script type="module" src="/src/main.js"></script>
  </body>
</html>
```

In *<div id="app"></div>* the App.vue component code will be injected.

Summary

In this chapter, we were introduced to Vue, a simple yet comprehensive JavaScript framework to make dynamic frontend UIs. We set up the environment (using Vite) to begin developing Vue apps and reviewed the purpose of certain files in a Vue project. In the next chapter, we will continue to see how to create and use Vue components.

CHAPTER 2: CREATING AND USING COMPONENTS

In the previous chapter, you learned about the core building blocks of Vue apps, components. In this chapter, we will implement a custom component from scratch to have an idea of what it is like to build a Vue app.

Creating our First Component

In VScode, open the project folder that you have created in chapter 1. In *src*, we have a folder *components* to store all our components (fig. 1).

Figure 1

In *components*, remove the default existing components *HelloWorld.vue*, *TheWelcome.vue*, *WelcomeItem.vue* as well as the *icons* folder. Create a new file *Products.vue* (fig. 1).

Note the naming convention of the file; we capitalize the first letter of the component *Products* followed by *.vue*.

Type out the below code into *Products.vue*:

Add Code

```
<script>
</script>
<template>
    <h1>Products</h1>
</template>
```

Our Products component simply outputs the string 'Products'.

Importing and Using our Created Component

A component can be used by other components. Let's import and add *<Products />* to /src/App.vue. Remove the existing codes in /src/App.vue and replace it with the below:

Replace Entire Code

```
<script>
import Products from './components/Products.vue';

export default{
  components:{
    Products
  }
}
</script>

<template>
      <Products />
</template>
```

Code Explanation

We first import *Products* component into *App* component using *import*:

Analyze Code

```
<script>
import Products from './components/Products.vue';
...
```

For importing custom components, we need to specify their path in the file system. Because Products Component is in the *components* folder, we import from './components/Products.vue'.
The path is relative to the current component path. './' means same folder. We use '../' to go back one folder and so on.

```
...
export default{
  components:{
    Products
  }
}
</script>
```

We register the *Products* component under the *components* option to make it available to App.

```
<template>
    <Products />
</template>
```

We then render the *Products* component in template. Now save App.vue and go to your browser. You should see the *Products* component markup displayed with the message (fig. 2)

Products

Figure 2

We have just referred to the *Products* component from App component. We can also render *Products* multiple times. Modify App.vue with the following in **bold**:

Modify Bold Code

```
...
<template>
  <Products />
  <Products />
  <Products />
</template>
```

You should see multiple Products component markup displayed (fig. 3):

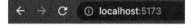

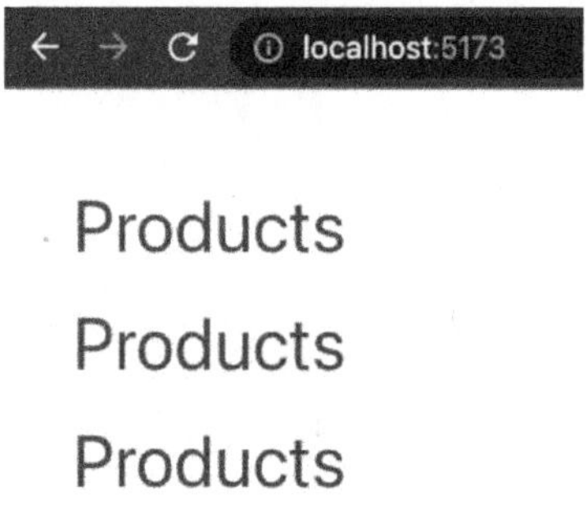

Products

Products

Products

Figure 3

Options API

Vue 3 components can be defined in with either Options API or Composition API. The Composition API aims to address code reusability and readability especially in larger applications. But in this book, we will be using the traditional Options API (available for both Vue 2 and Vue 3).

With Options API, we define a component's logic using options e.g. *data*, *methods* and *mounted*. Let's look at *data()* first. We will look at *methods* and *mounted* later.

data()

Suppose we have Products.vue as:

```
<script>
export default{
  data(){
      return{
        username: 'John',
        category: 'Books'
      }
  }
}
</script>
<template>
    <h1>Products: {{category}} by {{username}}</h1>
</template>
```

data() returns an object containing all the data we want Vue to work with. Any properties assigned to the returned object become *reactive*, meaning Vue observes them and automatically re-renders the UI when they change in value.

Properties returned from *data()* function can be exposed in <template> through text interpolation using the "Mustache" (double curly braces) syntax {{}}.

If we run the above, we have (fig. 4):

Products: Books by John

Figure 4

The mustache tag `<h1>Products: {{category}} by {{username}}</h1>` is replaced with the value of the *category* and *username* property from the component instance. The UI will be updated whenever *category* or *username* changes. This is known as declarative rendering where Vue allows you to declaratively bind the rendered DOM to the underlying component instance's data.

Essentially, properties returned from *data()* form the reactive state of the component. Whenever the properties in *data()* change, the DOM updates as well. We will revisit *data()* later.

Embedding JavaScript Expressions

You can also embed JavaScript expressions in <template> by wrapping them in double curly braces. Vue evaluates them before rendering. For example, we can do concatenation between variables:

Analyze Code
```
<template>
    <h1>{{ category + ' by ' + username }}</h1>
</template>
```

Conditional ternary expressions:

Analyze Code
```
<template>
    <h1>{{ username ? username : 'no username'}}</h1>
</template>
```

Displaying a List with Loops

We will illustrate displaying a list of products with loops in *Products*. In */src/components/Products.vue*, add the codes shown in **bold** below:

23

Modify Bold Code

```
<script>
export default{
  data(){
      return{
        products:[
            {
                id: "1",
                name: "airpods"
            },
            {
                id: "2",
                name: "kindle"
            },
            {
                id: "3",
                name: "keyboard"
            }
        ]
      }
  }
}
</script>
<template>
    <div v-for='product in products' :key='product.id'>
        <h3>{{product.id}}: {{product.name}}</h3>
    </div>
</template>
```

Back in /src/App.vue, make sure you render the *Products* component:

Modify Bold Code

```
<script>
import Products from './components/Products.vue';

export default{
  components:{
    Products
  }
}
</script>

<template>
    <Products />
</template>
```

Navigate to your browser and you should see the result in fig. 5.

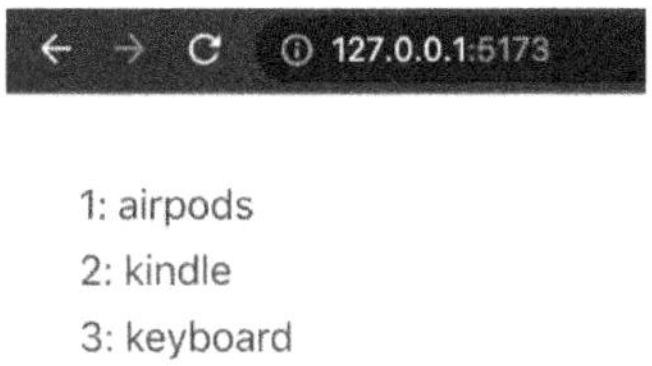

1: airpods

2: kindle

3: keyboard

Figure 5

Code Explanation

```
                            Analyze Code
export default{
  data(){
      return{
        products:[
              {
                  id: "1",
                  name: "airpods"
              },
              ...
          ]
      }
  }
}
</script>
```

First, in <script> of *Products component*, we declare an array *products* which contain the id and names of products.

```
                            Analyze Code
<template>
    <div v-for='product in products' :key='product.id'>
        <h3>{{product.id}}: {{product.name}}</h3>
    </div>
</template>
```

In template, we next use *v-for* to loop through each element in *products*. *v-for* requires a special syntax in the form of *product in products*, where *products* is the source data array and *product* is an alias for the array element being iterated on.

The v-for directive tells Vue that we want a section of our template to be rendered for every item in a collection. In our case, we output for each element:

Analyze Code
```
<h3>{{product.id}}: {{product.name}}</h3>
```

Note that we have provided a *key* attribute (*product.id*) for our product items. The key (product.id) tells Vue how to figure out which DOM node to change when *products* update. Thus, when dynamically editing the list, and removing/adding elements, you should always pass an identifier in lists to prevent issues.

Summary

You have learned a lot in this chapter. If you get stuck while following the code or if you would like to get the sample code we have used in this chapter, contact me at support@i-ducate.com.

In this chapter, we created our first custom component. We created a Products Component that retrieves product data from an array and renders that data (using the *v-for* loop) on the page. In the next chapter, we will explore props, data and events in Vue.

CHAPTER 3: BOOTSTRAP, V-BIND, PROPS, DATA AND EVENTS

In this chapter, we explore displaying data by binding controls in an HTML template to properties of a Vue component, how to apply CSS classes on styles dynamically, how to use the component properties and how to handle events raised from DOM elements.

Using the Bootstrap framework:

We will use *Bootstrap* to make our UI look more professional. Bootstrap (https://getbootstrap.com – fig. 1) is a library of reusable frontend components that contain HTML, CSS, and JavaScript-based templates to help build user interface components (like forms, buttons, icons) for web applications.

Figure 1

To get started with Bootstrap, we need to reference *bootstrap.css* in our *public/index.html*. Go to *getbootstrap.com* and scroll down to the 'Include via CDN' section.

Include via CDN

When you only need to include Bootstrap's compiled CSS or JS, you can use jsDelivr. See it in action with our simple quick start, or browse the examples to jumpstart your next project. You can also choose to include Popper and our JS separately.

```
<!-- CSS only -->
<link href="https://cdn.jsdelivr.net/npm/bootstrap@5.2.1/dist/css
```

```
<!-- JavaScript Bundle with Popper -->
<script src="https://cdn.jsdelivr.net/npm/bootstrap@5.2.1/dist/js
```

Figure 2

Copy the *bootstrap.min.css* stylesheet link and pass it into your *<head>* of *index.html*. (fig. 2). Note: as of book's writing, version of Bootstrap is v5.2.0.

Next, copy and paste the link of the *bootstrap.bundle.min.js* Bootstrap JS bundle before the body closing tag *</body>*:

```
<!DOCTYPE html>
<html lang="en">
  <head>
    <meta charset="UTF-8" />
    <link rel="icon" href="/favicon.ico" />
    <meta name="viewport" content="width=device-width, initial-scale=1.0" />
    <link
href="https://cdn.jsdelivr.net/npm/bootstrap@5.2.0/dist/css/bootstrap.min.css"
rel="stylesheet" integrity="…" crossorigin="anonymous">
    <title>Vite App</title>
  </head>
  <body>
    <div id="app"></div>
    <script type="module" src="/src/main.js"></script>
    <script
src="https://cdn.jsdelivr.net/npm/bootstrap@5.2.0/dist/js/bootstrap.bundle.min.js
" integrity="…" crossorigin="anonymous"></script>
  </body>
</html>
```

Test our App

Now, let's make sure that everything is working so far. Add a *Button* from Bootstrap (https://getbootstrap.com/docs/5.2/components/buttons/ - fig. 3).

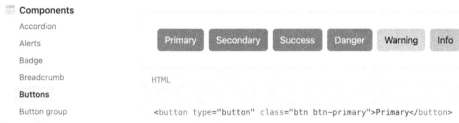

Figure 3

In App.vue, edit the code as highlighted in **bold**:

```
<script>
...
</script>

<template>
  <Products />
  <button type="button" class="btn btn-primary">Primary</button>
</template>
```

If you have successfully linked to Bootstrap, you should get your button displayed like in fig. 4.

Figure 4

There are times when we want to use different CSS classes on an element. For example, if we add the 'danger' button style as shown below:

```
                    Analyze Code
<button type="button" class="btn btn-danger">Danger</button>
```

we get the below button style (fig. 5).

Figure 5

29

And if I want to disable the button by applying the *disabled* class, I can do the following:

Analyze Code

```
<button type="button" class="btn btn-danger" disabled>Danger</button>
```

More information of styles of *button* and other components are available at the Bootstrap site under 'Components' (fig. 6).

Figure 6

Disabling Button on Condition using v-bind

Now, suppose I want to disable the button based on some condition. We can do the below:

Analyze Code

```
<script>
export default{
  data(){
    return{
      isValid: true
    }
  }
}
</script>

<template>
  <button type="button" class="btn btn-danger" v-bind:disabled="!isValid">
      Danger
  </button>
</template>
```

That is, when *isValid = false* the *disabled* CSS class will be applied, making the button unclickable. If *isValid = true* the *disabled* CSS class will not be applied, making the button clickable.

The *v-bind* directive keeps *disabled* in sync with the component's *isValid* property. We will be coming across v-bind so many times that it has a dedicated shorthand syntax ':'

```
<button type="button" class="…" :disabled="!isValid">Danger</button>
```

For the rest of the book, we will use the shorthand syntax in code examples. That's the most common usage for Vue developers.

* Directives with prefix *v-** indicate they are special attributes provided by Vue. They apply special reactive behavior to the rendered DOM (similar to Angular's *ng-** directives).

Props

We can pass data into a component by using 'props'. For example, suppose we want to display a list of products with their rating. We will need to pass the rating value to our rating component. We can do something like: *<Rating rating="4"/>* to display a rating of 4 stars.

To do so, in *src/components*, create a new file Rating.vue with the below code.

Add Code
```
<script>
export default{
    props: ['rating']
}
</script>
<template>
    <h1>Rating: {{rating}}</h1>
</template>
```

Our Rating component must declare a 'rating' prop using the *props* option. When a parent component renders *<Rating rating="4"/>*, the *rating* attribute will contain the value of 4. We then render the rating value in *template*.

In *src/App.vue*, replace the previous code with the following:

31

Replace Entire Code

```
<script>
import Rating from './components/Rating.vue';

export default{
  components:{
    Rating
  }
}
</script>

<template>
  <div>
      <Rating rating='1' />
      <Rating rating='2' />
      <Rating rating='3' />
      <Rating rating='4' />
      <Rating rating='5' />
  </div>
</template>
```

If you run your app, it should display something like (fig. 7):

Rating: 1

Rating: 2

Rating: 3

Rating: 4

Rating: 5

Figure 7

In App.vue, we first have `<Rating rating='1' />` . Vue calls the Rating component with *rating: '1'* as the props. Our Rating component outputs a *<h1>Rating: 1</h1>* as the result.

In this example, we pass in only one attribute as props. We can pass multiple attributes and even complex objects as props. We will illustrate this later in the book.

Improving the Look

We will improve the look of our rating component by showing rating stars like what we see on Amazon.com instead of showing the rating value numerically. A user can click select from a rating of one star to five stars. We will implement this as a component and reuse it in many places. For now, don't worry about calling a server or any other logic. We just want to implement the UI first.

To show rating stars instead of just number values, we will use Bootstrap Icons (fig. 8) from *https://icons.getbootstrap.com/*.

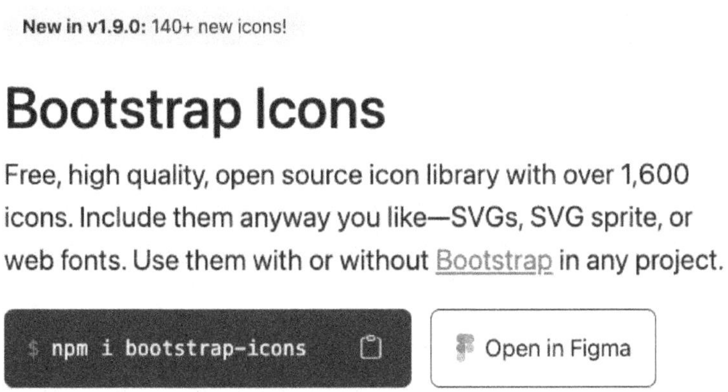

New in v1.9.0: 140+ new icons!

Bootstrap Icons

Free, high quality, open source icon library with over 1,600 icons. Include them anyway you like—SVGs, SVG sprite, or web fonts. Use them with or without Bootstrap in any project.

```
$ npm i bootstrap-icons
```

Open in Figma

Figure 8

Note: To use Bootstrap icons, run in the Terminal:

```
npm i bootstrap-icons
```

And include the icon fonts stylesheet in <head> of index.html (fig. 9):

CDN

Include the icon fonts stylesheet—in your website <head> or via @import in CSS—from our CDN and get started in seconds. See icon font docs for examples.

```
<link rel="stylesheet" href="https
```

Figure 9

index.html

```
<!DOCTYPE html>
<html lang="en">
  <head>
      ...
    <link rel="stylesheet" href="https://cdn.jsdelivr.net/npm/bootstrap-
icons@1.9.1/font/bootstrap-icons.css">
    <title>Vite App</title>
  </head>
```

We will be using the *star* and *star-fill* icons (fig. 10):

Figure 10

To include them in our project, add the below codes in **bold** into Rating component:

```
                        Modify Bold Code
<script>
export default{
    props: ['rating']
}
</script>
<template>
    <h1>Rating: {{rating}}</h1>
    <i v-if="rating >=1" class="bi bi-star-fill"></i>
    <i v-else class="bi bi-star"></i>
    <i v-if="rating >=2" class="bi bi-star-fill"></i>
    <i v-else class="bi bi-star"></i>
    <i v-if="rating >=3" class="bi bi-star-fill"></i>
    <i v-else class="bi bi-star"></i>
    <i v-if="rating >=4" class="bi bi-star-fill"></i>
    <i v-else class="bi bi-star"></i>
    <i v-if="rating >=5" class="bi bi-star-fill"></i>
    <i v-else class="bi bi-star"></i>
</template>
```

Code Explanation - Conditional Rendering

We render the *star* and *star-fill* icons with:

Analyze Code

```
<i v-if="rating >=1" class="bi bi-star-fill"></i>
<i v-else class="bi bi-star"></i>
```

We use the *v-if* directive to conditionally render a filled star if *rating is >= 1*. Else, render a normal (empty) star with the *v-else* counterpart.
The *v-if* block will only be rendered if the expression (e.g. *rating* >= 1) returns true.

The above code is for the first star. The remaining similar repetitions are for the four remaining stars. However, note the change in value of each condition depending on which star it is. For example, the second star's condition should be

Analyze Code

```
<i v-if="rating >=2" class="bi bi-star-fill"></i>
<i v-else class="bi bi-star"></i>
```

The second star should be empty if the rating is less than two. It should be filled if the rating is more than or equal to two. The same goes for the third, fourth and fifth star.

Running your App

When we run our app, we get the icons displayed (fig. 11):

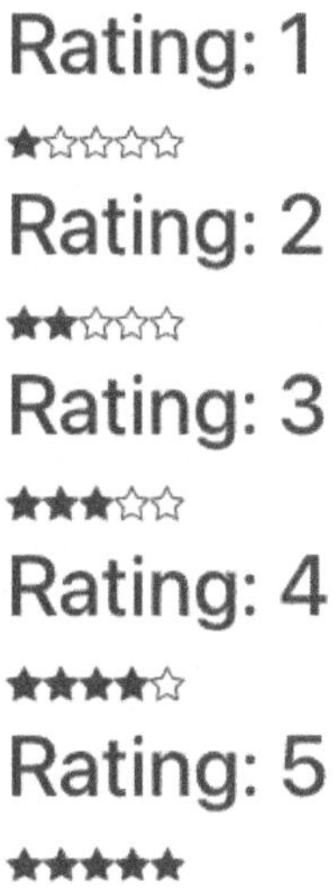

Rating: 1
★☆☆☆☆

Rating: 2
★★☆☆☆

Rating: 3
★★★☆☆

Rating: 4
★★★★☆

Rating: 5
★★★★★

Figure 11

Data in a Vue Component

Every component in addition to having its own template, styles and logic, manages its own reactive data using the *data* option. For example, Rating component can have a reactive data variable *rating* to store the rating value:

```
                          Analyze Code
<script>
export default{
    props: ['rating'],
    data(){
        return{
            rating: 0
        }
    }
}
</script>
```

Whenever the reactive data changes, the UI is re-rendered to reflect those changes. We often refer to this as the component or local state.

Now, we have an issue in that we have a *rating* prop and also *rating* variable in the state. Let's rename the *rating* prop to *initialRating* to better reflect its purpose (since it's the initial rating assigned when we first create the Rating instance).

```
export default{
    props: ['initialRating'],
```

In App.vue, change *rating* to *initialRating*:

```
        <Rating initialRating='1' />
        <Rating initialRating='2' />
        <Rating initialRating='3' />
        <Rating initialRating='4' />
        <Rating initialRating='5' />
```

Note that props cannot be mutated. In Rating, our prop *initialRating* is used to pass in an initial rating value from the parent. We then assign the value of *initialRating* to the *rating* state variable in *data()*:

36

Rating.vue

```
<script>
export default{
    props: ['initialRating'],
    data(){
        return{
    // rating only uses this.initialRating as the initial value;
    // it is disconnected from future prop updates.
            rating: this.initialRating
        }
    }
}
</script>
```

Now, suppose we want our user to be able to change the rating by clicking on the specified star. How do we make our rating component render in response to a user click?

Handling Events

Next, we want to assign a rating depending on which star the user has clicked. To do so, our component needs to handle the click event. In Vue, you can define a listener for a DOM event in the template using the *v-on* directive (typically shortened to the @ symbol).

For example, to make our rating component handle user clicks, we specify the *v-on:click* attribute with a method:

Rating.vue

```
                        Modify Bold Code
<script>
export default{
    props: ['initialRating'],
    data(){
        return{
            rating: this.initialRating
        }
    },
    methods:{
        assignRating(rating){
            this.rating = rating
        }
    }
}
</script>
```

```
<template>
    <h1>Rating: {{rating}}</h1>
    <span v-on:click="assignRating(1)">
        <i v-if="rating >=1" class="bi bi-star-fill"></i>
        <i v-else class="bi bi-star"></i>
    </span>
    <span v-on:click="assignRating(2)">
        <i v-if="rating >=2" class="bi bi-star-fill"></i>
        <i v-else class="bi bi-star"></i>
    </span>
    <span v-on:click="assignRating(3)">
        <i v-if="rating >=3" class="bi bi-star-fill"></i>
        <i v-else class="bi bi-star"></i>
    </span>
    <span v-on:click="assignRating(4)">
        <i v-if="rating >=4" class="bi bi-star-fill"></i>
        <i v-else class="bi bi-star"></i>
    </span>
    <span v-on:click="assignRating(5)">
        <i v-if="rating >=5" class="bi bi-star-fill"></i>
        <i v-else class="bi bi-star"></i>
    </span>
</template>
```

Code Explanation

We wrap each star's *v-if, v-else* clause in a *span* element and pass in *assignRating* as the method handling the *click* event.

We add custom methods to a component in the *methods* option:

```
export default{
    ...
    methods:{
        assignRating(rating){
            this.rating = rating
        }
    }
}
```

* Having methods in the *methods* option helps keep our UI logic together and out of the template. This keeps the template clean and readable.

The methods are accessible in the component's template. They are commonly used as event listeners. Thus, we have: *<span v-on:click="assignRating(1)">* to assign a rating of one if a user clicks on this star.

We then change the value of the argument to *assignRating* depending on which star it is. The second star's *v-on:click* should be *<span v-on:click="assignRating(2)">*.

So, when a user clicks on the second star, *rating* is assigned with value of two. When a user clicks on the third star, *rating* is assigned value of three and so on.

Remember that whenever a reactive data variable has a new value assigned to it, our component automatically re-renders thus showing the updated value on to the view.

Running your App

When you run your app now, you should be able to see your ratings and also adjust their values by clicking on the specified star (fig. 12).

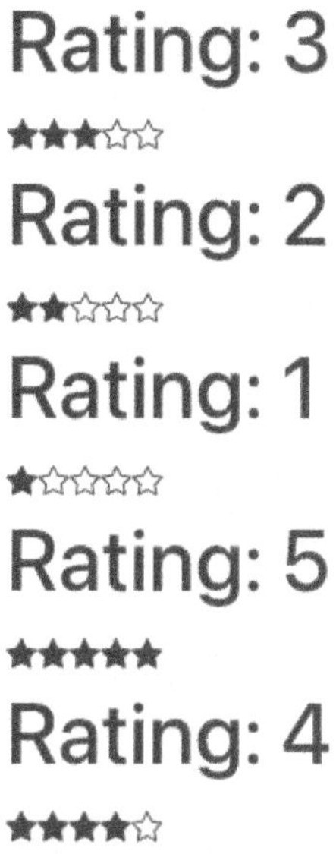

Rating: 3
★★★☆☆
Rating: 2
★★☆☆☆
Rating: 1
★☆☆☆☆
Rating: 5
★★★★★
Rating: 4
★★★★☆

Figure 12

Note that we have five different rating components each having their own local state. Each updates independently. Each rating component does not affect another rating component's state.

Summary

In this chapter, we learned about binding controls in a HTML template to Vue component properties, using the component data and handling events raised from DOM elements. We used Bootstrap to make our UI more professional. In the next chapter, we will see how to put multiple components together in an application.

Contact me at support@i-ducate.com for the full source code of this chapter or if you encounter any errors with your code.

CHAPTER 4: WORKING WITH COMPONENTS

In this chapter, we will learn more about using components, how to reuse them and put them together in an application. Execute the codes in the following sections in your existing project from chapter three.

Styles

We can further modify our components with our own CSS styles. These *styles* are scoped only to your component. They won't effect to the outer DOM or other components.

To illustrate, suppose we want our filled stars to be orange, in src/components/Rating.vue we add the following in **bold**:

Modify Bold Code
```
export default{
    props: ['initialRating'],
    data(){
        return{
            rating: this.initialRating,
            color: 'orange'
        }
    },
...
```

We create a new reactive state variable *color* to contain the style color. If required, you can further specify other styling properties like *height*, *backgroundColor*, *fontSize* etc.

To apply this style, add the below *style* binding:

Modify Bold Code
```
...
    <h1>Rating: {{rating}}</h1>
    <span :style="{color: color}" v-on:click="assignRating(1)">
        <i v-if="rating >=1" class="bi bi-star-fill"></i>
        <i v-else class="bi bi-star"></i>
    </span>
...
```

:style corresponds to an HTML element's *style* property and supports binding to a JavaScript object.

Do the same for the rest of the stars. When we run our application, we will see our filled stars with the orange CSS applied to it (fig. 1).

41

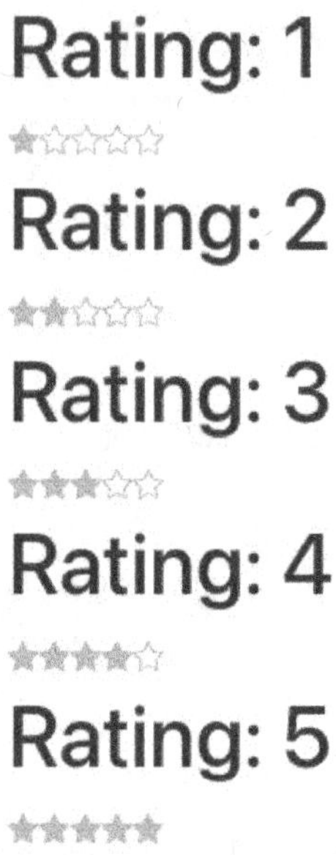

Rating: 1

★☆☆☆☆

Rating: 2

★★☆☆☆

Rating: 3

★★★☆☆

Rating: 4

★★★★☆

Rating: 5

★★★★★

Figure 1

And if we re-assign blue to *color*,

```
                            Analyze Code
    data(){
        return{
            rating: this.initialRating,
            color: 'blue'
        }
    },
...
```

We get:

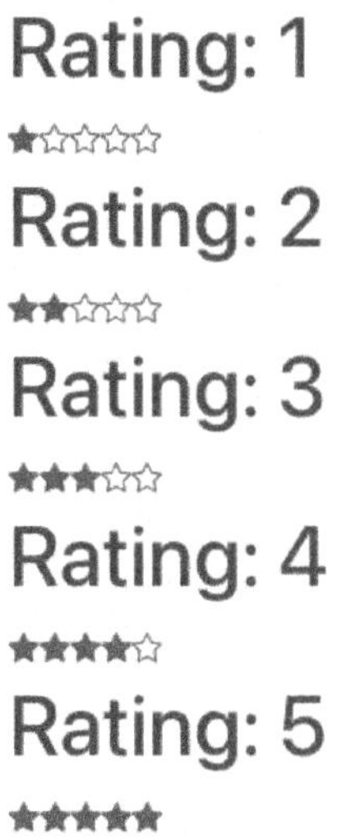

Rating: 1

★☆☆☆☆

Rating: 2

★★☆☆☆

Rating: 3

★★★☆☆

Rating: 4

★★★★☆

Rating: 5

★★★★★

Figure 2

4.2 Example Application

We will reuse the rating component that we have made and implement a product listing like in figure 3.

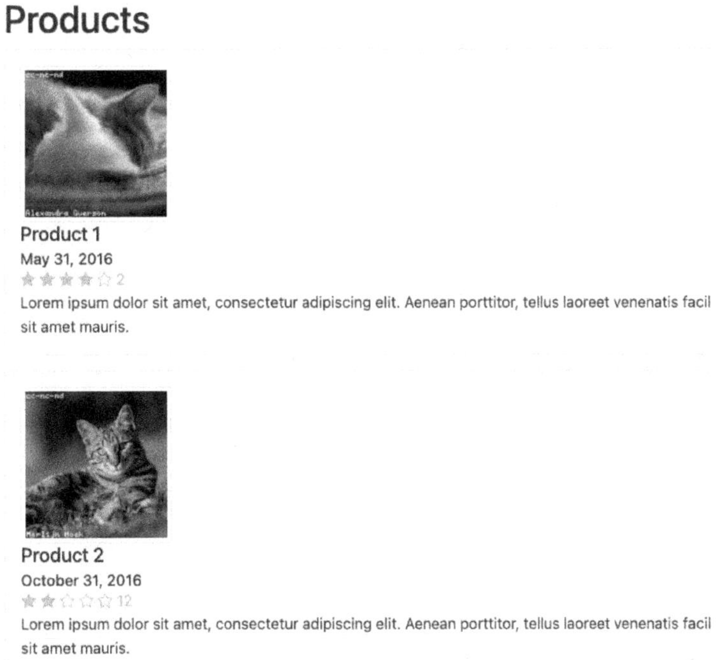

Products

Product 1
May 31, 2016
★ ★ ★ ★ ☆ 2
Lorem ipsum dolor sit amet, consectetur adipiscing elit. Aenean porttitor, tellus laoreet venenatis facil
sit amet mauris.

Product 2
October 31, 2016
★ ★ ☆ ☆ ☆ 12
Lorem ipsum dolor sit amet, consectetur adipiscing elit. Aenean porttitor, tellus laoreet venenatis facil
sit amet mauris.

Figure 3

This is like the list of products on Amazon. For each product, we have an image, the product name, the product release date, the rating component and the number of ratings it has.

In *src/components*, create a new component file *Product.vue* that contains the Product Component. This component will be used to render one product.

How do we get our template to render each product listing like in figure 2? We use the *Card Horizontal* component in Bootstrap. Go to https://getbootstrap.com/docs/5.2/components/card/#horizontal (fig. 4).

Horizontal

Using a combination of grid and utility classes, cards can be made horizontal in a mobile-friendly and responsive way. In the example below, we remove the grid gutters with `.g-0` and use `.col-md-*` classes to make the card horizontal at the md breakpoint. Further adjustments may be needed depending on your card content.

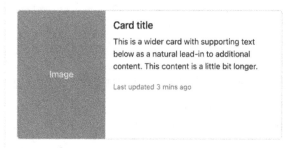

Card title

This is a wider card with supporting text below as a natural lead-in to additional content. This content is a little bit longer.

Last updated 3 mins ago

Figure 4

Copy the below slightly modified and simplified markup into *Product.vue* (check that it is *Product.vue* and not *Products.vue*) markup:

Add Code

```
<script>
import Rating from './Rating.vue';

export default{
    props: {
        data: Object
    },
    components:{
        Rating
    }
}
</script>
<template>
```

44

```
    <div class="card mb-3" style="max-width: 540px;">
    <div class="row g-0">
        <div class="col-md-4">
        <img :src="data.imageUrl" class="img-fluid rounded-start"
alt="...">
        </div>
        <div class="col-md-8">
        <div class="card-body">
            <h5 class="card-title">{{data.productName}}</h5>
            <Rating :initialRating='data.rating' />
            <p class="card-text">{{data.description}}</p>
            <p class="card-text"><small class="text-muted">
            {{data.releasedDate}}</small>
            </p>
        </div>
        </div>
    </div>
    </div>
</template>
```

Code Explanation

```
import Rating from './Rating.vue';
```

We first import *Rating* component.

Next, in the markup, notice that to assign values of our product, we used props to inject the values (indicated in **bold**). Our Product component is expecting a *props data* object with the fields: *imageUrl*, *productName*, *releasedDate*, *description* and *rating*.

We have also added our rating component that expects input rating.

Analyze Code
```
<Rating :initialRating='data.rating' />
```

Products.vue

Next in *src/components/Products.vue*, declare a *products* array that contains a list of products. Type in the below code (or copy it from the source code) into *Products.vue*.

Replace Entire Code

```
<script>
import Product from './Product.vue';

export default{
  components:{
    Product
  },
  data(){
      return{
        products:[
            {
                id: '1',
                imageUrl: "http://loremflickr.com/150/150?random=1",
                productName: "Product 1",
                releasedDate: "May 31, 2016",
                description: "Lorem ipsum dolor sit amet, consectetur..",
                rating: 4
            },
            {
                id: '2',
                imageUrl: "http://loremflickr.com/150/150?random=2",
                productName: "Product 2",
                releasedDate: "October 31, 2016",
                description: "Lorem ipsum dolor sit amet, consectetur..",
                rating: 2
            },
            {
                id: '3',
                imageUrl: "http://loremflickr.com/150/150?random=3",
                productName: "Product 3",
                releasedDate: "July 30, 2016",
                description: "Lorem ipsum dolor sit amet, consectetur..",
                rating: 5
            }
        ]
      }
  }
}
</script>
<template>
    <div v-for='product in products' :key='product.id'>
        <Product :data="product" />
    </div>
</template>
```

Notice that in our component, we currently hardcode an array of product objects. Later on, we will

46

explore how to receive data from a server.

For *imageUrl*, we use http://loremflickr.com/150/150?random=1 to render a random image 150 pixels by 150 pixels. For multiple product images, we change the query string parameter *random=2, 3,4* and so on to get a different random image.

The code in *<template>* is similar to the one in chapter three where we loop through the names in *products* array to list them. This time however, our element is not just simple strings but a *data* object which contains Product properties *imageUrl*, *productName*, *releasedDate*, *description* and *rating*.

Lastly in *src/App.vue*, make sure you import and render your *Products* component:

Replace Entire Code

```
<script>
import Products from './components/Products.vue';

export default{
  components:{
    Products
  }
}
</script>

<template>
  <div>
    <Products />
  </div>
</template>
```

Save all your files and you should have your application running fine like in figure 5.

Product 1

★★★★☆

Lorem ipsum dolor sit amet, consectetur..

May 31, 2016

Product 2

★★☆☆☆

Lorem ipsum dolor sit amet, consectetur..

October 31, 2016

Figure 5

Summary

In this chapter, we illustrate how to modify CSS styles taken from Bootstrap and reusing components to put them together in our example Product Listing application.

Contact me at support@i-ducate.com if you encounter any issues or for the full source code of this chapter.

CHAPTER 5: BUILDING FORMS

In this chapter, we look at how to implement forms with validation logic in Vue. As an example, we will implement a login form that takes in fields *email* and *password*.

Create an Initial Form Template

In your existing project from chapter 4, in *src/components* folder create a new file *UserForm.vue* and copy-paste the default form template from Bootstrap (https://getbootstrap.com/docs/5.2/forms/overview/ - fig. 1) into it:

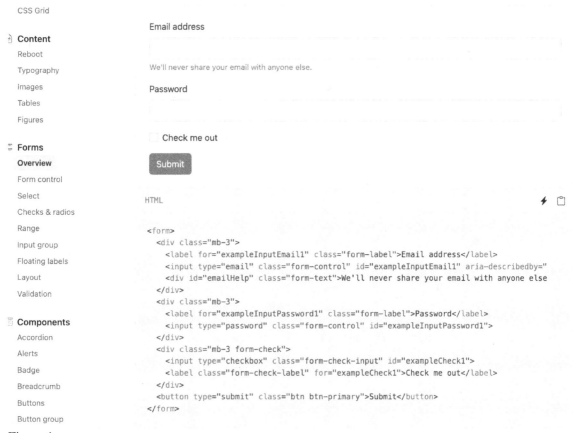

Figure 1

Add Code

```
<script>
export default{
}
</script>
<template>
<form>
  <div class="mb-3">
    <label for="exampleInputEmail1" class="form-label">
        Email address
    </label>
    <input type="email" class="form-control">
  </div>
  <div class="mb-3">
    <label for="exampleInputPassword1" class="form-label">
        Password
    </label>
    <input type="password" class="form-control">
  </div>
  <button type="submit" class="btn btn-primary">Submit</button>
</form>
</template>
```

Note: to simplify things, I've removed the:
- *checkbox* input
- *id* attributes for the *inputs*
- *emailHelp* element

Running the Form

We can try running the form by rendering *UserForm* in App.vue:

Replace Entire Code

```
<script>
import UserForm from './components/UserForm.vue';

export default{
  components:{
    UserForm
  }
}
</script>

<template>
    <UserForm />
</template>
```

50

And it should look something like:

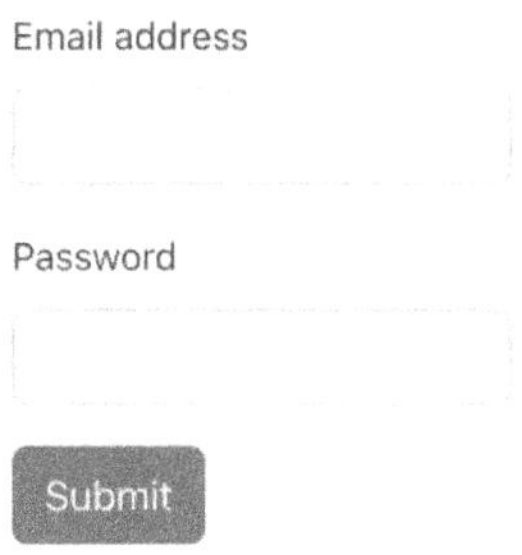

Email address

Password

Submit

Figure 2

Form Input Bindings

In Vue forms, we use the *v-model* directive to sync (two-way bind) the form input elements with the component's *data* property. Changes to the input updates the *data* property.

In src/components/UserForm.vue, add in the below lines in **bold**:

Modify Bold Code

```
<script>
export default{
    data(){
        return{
            email:'',
            password:''
        }
    }
}
</script>
<template>
<form>
  <div class="mb-3">
    <label for="exampleInputEmail1" class="form-label">
        Email address
    </label>
    <input v-model="email" type="email" class="form-control">
  </div>
  <div class="mb-3">
    <label for="exampleInputPassword1" class="form-label">
        Password
    </label>
    <input v-model="password" type="password" class="form-control">
```

```
  </div>
  <button type="submit" class="btn btn-primary">Submit</button>
</form>
<br>
<div class="card">
  <div class="card-body">
    Email: {{email}}
    <br>
    Password: {{password}}
  </div>
</div>
</template>
```

Code Explanation

```
data(){
    return{
        email:'',
        password:''
    }
}
```

We declare two properties *email* and *password* and set their initial value to an empty string ".

To bind the *email* property to the email input, we have **v-model="email"**. This creates a two-way binding between the data and the UI. If *email* changes, the input field will update its value.
The opposite is true as well. If the form is updated by the user, the *email* variable value changes.
The same applies for **v-model="password".**

We illustrate this by displaying the values below the form by adding:

Analyze Code

```
...
</form>
<br>
<div class="card">
  <div class="card-body">
    Email: {{email}}
    <br>
    Password: {{password}}
  </div>
</div>
</template>
```

When we run the app, we should see the values displayed at the bottom of the form like:

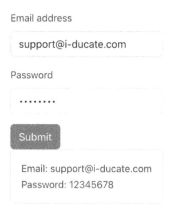

Figure 3

Showing Specific Validation Errors

Currently, we have the default email validation. But we should be able to have specific validation errors depending on the input given, for example "Email is required", or "Email should be a minimum of six characters" and show corresponding validation error alerts when a user submits the form.

To show specific validation errors, we declare two data variables to store our email and password error messages, and two Booleans to state if email and password fields are valid. In UserForm.vue, add the following code:

```
                        Modify Bold Code
<script>
export default{
    data(){
        return{
            email:'',
            password:'',
            validEmail: false,
            validPassword: false,
            emailMessage: '',
            passwordMessage: ''
        }
    },
...
```

To handle form submission, we define a *onSubmit* handling method. We then bind *onSubmit* to the *submit* event handler in the *form* element. Add the below codes in **bold**:

Modify Bold Code

```
<script>
export default{
    data(){
        ...
    },
    methods:{
        onSubmit(){
            if(this.validEmail){
                alert('Email: ' + this.email + '\nPassword: ' +
    this.password);
            }
        }
    }
}
</script>

<template>
<form @submit.prevent="onSubmit">
...
```

When the form is submitted, *onSubmit* will be called.

*Note that we specify *@submit.prevent* in the <form> tag to prevent the submit event from reloading the page when we send the contents of the form (our app is an SPA that dynamically updates the current web page with new data without page reloading).

In a normal app, we will want to send the form to some external API e.g. login. Before we send the network request in *onSubmit*, we want to perform some client-side validation. For example, if *username* length is zero, if it's less than a minimum length, if there are spaces in between etc. We illustrate this for the *email* field by adding an *if-else-if*.

Modify Bold Code

```
...
    methods:{
        onSubmit(e){
            this.validEmail = false;
            if(this.email.length < 6){
                this.emailMessage = "Email should be minimum 6
characters";
            }
            else if(this.email.indexOf(' ') >= 0){
                this.emailMessage = 'Email cannot contain spaces';
            }
            else{
                this.emailMessage = '';
```

54

```
            this.validEmail = true;
        }

        if(this.validEmail){
            alert('Email: ' + this.email + '\nPassword: ' +
this.password);
        }
        else{
            alert(this.emailMessage)
        }
    }
}
...
```

For each *if*-clause, we check for a specific validation, and if so, assign the specific error message to *emailMessage*. Only when it manages to reach the last *else* clause that we know we have no email validation errors and we set *validEmail* to true and *emailMessage* to an empty string.

And if *validEmail* is true, we then show an alert with what has been entered into the form.

Running your App

When you run your app, fill in a valid email and click on submit. An alert box appears with the inputted values (fig. 4).

Figure 4

Let's repeat the above steps for the *password* field. We add an *if-else-if* for *password* similar to *email*.

Modify Bold Code

```
...
        onSubmit(e){
            this.validEmail = false;
            ...
            ...
            ...

            this.validPassword = false;
            if(this.password.length < 6){
                this.passwordMessage = "Password should be minimum 6
characters";
            }
            else if(this.password.indexOf(' ') >= 0){
                this.passwordMessage = "Password cannot contain spaces";
            }
            else{
                this.passwordMessage = '';
                this.validPassword = true;
            }

            if(this.validEmail && this.validPassword){
                alert('Email: ' + this.email + '\nPassword: ' +
this.password);
            }
            else{
                alert(this.emailMessage + '\n' + this.passwordMessage)
            }
        }
...
```

In *onSubmit*, we add the check for a valid password as well.

When you run your app now, the submission will only be successful when both email and password fields have valid values.

In a normal app, instead of showing an alert, we will usually send the data in a request to some API. We illustrate this in a later chapter.

Showing Validation Error Messages

Now, if we enter an invalid email address or password, our form doesn't submit because of the validation checks we have added in. But we should be showing validation errors to the user for her to correct her input. We will do that in this section.

We will use the *Alert* component from Bootstrap to provide feedback messages (fig. 5).

Examples

Alerts are available for any length of text, as well as an optional close button. For proper styling, use one of the eight **required** contextual classes (e.g., `.alert-success`). For inline dismissal, use the alerts JavaScript plugin.

A simple primary alert—check it out!

A simple secondary alert—check it out!

A simple success alert—check it out!

A simple danger alert—check it out!

A simple warning alert—check it out!

Figure 5

We add the *Alert* below our email and password input fields:

Modify Bold Code

```
...
<form @submit.prevent="onSubmit">
  <div class="mb-3">
    <label for="exampleInputEmail1" class="form-label">
        Email address
    </label>
    <input v-model="email" type="email" class="form-control">
  </div>
  <div v-if="emailMessage.length > 0" class="alert alert-danger"
role="alert">
    {{ emailMessage }}
  </div>
  <div class="mb-3">
    <label for="exampleInputPassword1" class="form-label">
        Password
    </label>
    <input v-model="password" type="password" class="form-control">
  </div>
  <div v-if="passwordMessage.length > 0" class="alert alert-danger"
role="alert">
    {{ passwordMessage }}
  </div>
  <button type="submit" class="btn btn-primary">Submit</button>
</form>
```

...

Using *v-if*, we include a condition in *Alert*. We show the error message only if the error message's length is more than 0, indicating that there is an error.

If we run our app now and submit with an email less than 6 characters and a password with spaces, we get (fig. 6):

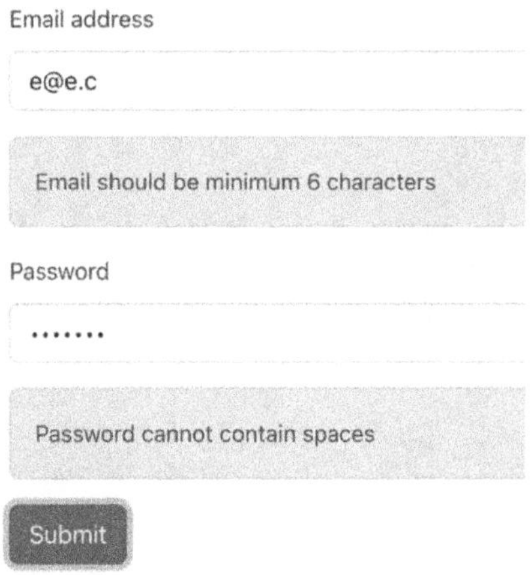

Email address

e@e.c

Email should be minimum 6 characters

Password

•••••••

Password cannot contain spaces

Submit

Figure 6

See how you can extend your application with more validation checks?

Clearing the Fields Upon Successful Submit

Currently, after submitting our forms, the user-entered values in the fields remain. They should be cleared after submission. To do so, in *onSubmit*, after successful validation, we clear the *email* and *password* state and also set *validEmail* and *validPassword* to false:

Modify Bold Code

...

```
if(this.validEmail && this.validPassword){
    this.email = "";
    this.password = "";
    this.validEmail = false;
    this.validPassword = false;
}
else{
    alert(this.emailMessage + '\n' + this.passwordMessage)
}
```

...

58

Now, when you run your app again and submit the form, because the field values are binded to the state's, the fields will be cleared out.

Exercise

Now that we have completed our login form, try to come up with your own form and have additional inputs like text-areas, check boxes, radio buttons and more. The markup for them is available at *https://getbootstrap.com/docs/5.2/forms/overview/*. They all work similar to the input fields that we have gone through.

Complete Code

We have covered a lot about Vue Forms in this chapter. Below lists the complete code for *UserForm.vue* which is also available in my source code.

Analyze Code

```
<script>
export default{
    data(){
        return{
            email:'',
            password:'',
            validEmail: false,
            validPassword: false,
            emailMessage: '',
            passwordMessage: ''
        }
    },
    methods:{
        onSubmit(){
            this.validEmail = false;
            if(this.email.length < 6){
                this.emailMessage = "Email should be minimum 6 characters";
            }
            else if(this.email.indexOf(' ') >= 0){
                this.emailMessage = 'Email cannot contain spaces';
            }
            else{
                this.emailMessage = '';
                this.validEmail = true;
            }

            this.validPassword = false;
            if(this.password.length < 6){
                this.passwordMessage = "Password should be minimum 6 characters";
            }
            else if(this.password.indexOf(' ') >= 0){
```

```
                this.passwordMessage = "Password cannot contain spaces";
            }
            else{
                this.passwordMessage = '';
                this.validPassword = true;
            }

            if(this.validEmail && this.validPassword){
                this.email = "";
                this.password = "";
                this.validEmail = false;
                this.validPassword = false;
            }
            else{
                alert(this.emailMessage + '\n' + this.passwordMessage)
            }
        }
    }
}
</script>
<template>
<form @submit.prevent="onSubmit">
  <div class="mb-3">
    <label for="exampleInputEmail1" class="form-label">
        Email address
    </label>
    <input v-model="email" type="email" class="form-control">
  </div>
  <div v-if="emailMessage.length > 0" class="alert alert-danger" role="alert">
    {{ emailMessage }}
  </div>
  <div class="mb-3">
    <label for="exampleInputPassword1" class="form-label">
        Password
    </label>
    <input v-model="password" type="password" class="form-control">
  </div>
  <div v-if="passwordMessage.length > 0" class="alert alert-danger" role="alert">
    {{ passwordMessage }}
  </div>
  <button type="submit" class="btn btn-primary">Submit</button>
</form>
<br>
<div class="card">
  <div class="card-body">
    Email: {{email}}
    <br>
    Password: {{password}}
  </div>
</div>
</template>
```

Summary

In this chapter, we learnt how to create a form with validation logic. We created an initial form with template from BootStrap. We learned how to use *v-bind* to bind component data variables to form fields. We used JavaScript functions to handle form submission.

We showed form specific form field validation errors and how to validate the form upon submission.

Now after submitting a form, we need to persist the data by calling the API endpoint of the server. We will explore how to communicate with the server in a later chapter.

Contact support@i-ducate.com if you have not already had the full source code for this chapter.

CHAPTER 6: GETTING DATA FROM RESTFUL APIS

In this chapter, we will see how to call backend services to get data through RESTful APIs.

You can work in your existing project from chapter 5 or create a new project.

GitHub RESTful API

Building RESTful APIs is beyond the scope of Vue because Vue is a client-side technology whereas building RESTful APIs require server-side technology like NodeJS, Django, ASP.NET, and so on. (I have written books on NodeJS and Django. Contact support@i-ducate.com if you are interested).

We will illustrate by connecting to the GitHub RESTful API to retrieve and manage GitHub content. You can know more about the GitHub API at

```
https://developer.github.com/v3/
```

But as a quick introduction, we can get GitHub users data with the following URL,

```
https://api.github.com/search/users?q=<search term>
```

We simply specify our search term in the URL to get GitHub data for user with name matching our search term. An example is shown below with search term *greg*.

```
https://api.github.com/search/users?q=greg
```

When we make a call to this URL, we will get the following JSON objects as a result (fig. 1).

```
api.github.com/search/users?q=greg

{
  "total_count": 37894,
  "incomplete_results": false,
  "items": [
    {
      "login": "greg",
      "id": 1658846,
      "node_id": "MDQ6VXNlcjE2NTg4NDY=",
      "avatar_url": "https://avatars.githubusercontent.com/u/1658846?v=4",
      "gravatar_id": "",
      "url": "https://api.github.com/users/greg",
      "html_url": "https://github.com/greg",
      "followers_url": "https://api.github.com/users/greg/followers",
      "following_url": "https://api.github.com/users/greg/following{/other_user}",
      "gists_url": "https://api.github.com/users/greg/gists{/gist_id}",
      "starred_url": "https://api.github.com/users/greg/starred{/owner}{/repo}",
      "subscriptions_url": "https://api.github.com/users/greg/subscriptions",
      "organizations_url": "https://api.github.com/users/greg/orgs",
      "repos_url": "https://api.github.com/users/greg/repos",
      "events_url": "https://api.github.com/users/greg/events{/privacy}",
      "received_events_url": "https://api.github.com/users/greg/received_events",
      "type": "User",
      "site_admin": false,
      "score": 1.0
    },
    {
      "login": "gregkh",
      "id": 14953,
      "node_id": "MDQ6VXNlcjE0OTUz",
      "avatar_url": "https://avatars.githubusercontent.com/u/14953?v=4",
      "gravatar_id": "",
      "url": "https://api.github.com/users/gregkh",
      "html_url": "https://github.com/gregkh",
      "followers_url": "https://api.github.com/users/gregkh/followers",
      "following_url": "https://api.github.com/users/gregkh/following{/other_user}",
      "gists_url": "https://api.github.com/users/gregkh/gists{/gist_id}",
      "starred_url": "https://api.github.com/users/gregkh/starred{/owner}{/repo}",
      "subscriptions_url": "https://api.github.com/users/gregkh/subscriptions",
      "organizations_url": "https://api.github.com/users/gregkh/orgs",
      "repos_url": "https://api.github.com/users/gregkh/repos",
      "events_url": "https://api.github.com/users/gregkh/events{/privacy}",
      "received_events_url": "https://api.github.com/users/gregkh/received_events",
      "type": "User",
      "site_admin": false,
      "score": 1.0
    },
```

Figure 1

Getting Data

To get data using a RESTful API, we are going to use the *fetch()* method.

To begin, in *src/components* folder, create a new file GitHub.vue with the below code.

Add Code

```
<script>
export default{
    methods:{
        async fetchGitHubUsers(){
            const res = await fetch(
                'https://api.github.com/search/users?q=greg')
```

```
            const data = await res.json()
            console.log(data.items);
        }
    },
    async created(){
        this.fetchGitHubUsers()
    }
}
</script>
```

Code Explanation

In *created*, we call *fetchGitHubUsers*. *fetchGitHubUsers* returns GitHub data from our API endpoint. We will later explain what's *created*. We first dwell into the code inside *fetchGitHubUsers*.

In *fetch*, we call the GitHub API with argument 'greg'.

Analyze Code
```
        const res = await fetch(
            'https://api.github.com/search/users?q=greg')
```

fetch returns a *promise* which we subscribe to using *async/await* so that the code reads like synchronous code:

Analyze Code
```
    async fetchGitHubUsers(){
        const res = await fetch(
            'https://api.github.com/search/users?q=greg')

        const data = await res.json()
        console.log(data.items);
    }
```

Actions after the *await* keyword are not executed until the promise resolves, meaning the code will wait. When we use *await*, we have to add *async* to the method declaring that it is making the request as an asynchronous function.

After *await*, we have *console.log(data.items)*. Note that we access *data.items* property to get the *items* array direct as that is the JSON structure of the GitHub response. So when our AJAX call is completed, we print the list of items returned which is the GitHub users search results.

created()

Now what's *created()*? And why do we place our data request and retrieval code in it?

Every Vue component instance fires several lifecycle events we can hook on (add and run our own code at specific stages). The methods you will probably find yourself using most often are:

- *created*. This is the place to kick off any requests for fetching data from APIs. Thus, we place our data retrieval code here.
- *mounted* is fired after the component has been rendered and inserted into the DOM. This is where you can manipulate the DOM elements.
- *beforeUnmount*. This method is called just before the component is removed from the DOM. You can do any cleanup here.

Running our App

Before we run our app, remember that we have to import and call our GitHub component in App.vue.

Replace Entire Code

```
<script>
import GitHub from './components/GitHub.vue';

export default{
  components:{
    GitHub
  }
}
</script>

<template>
    <GitHub />
</template>
```

Now run your app in Chrome. Go to 'View', 'Developer', 'Developer Tools'. Under console, you can see the following result from the console (fig. 2).

Figure 2

Our requested JSON object is a single object containing an items array of size 30 with each item representing the data of a GitHub user.

Each *user* object has properties *avatar_url*, *html_url*, *login*, *score*, and so on (fig. 3).

```
(30) [{...}, {...}, {...}, {...}, {...}, {...}, {...}, {...}, {...}, {...}, {...}, {...}, {...}, {
    {...}, {...}, {...}, {...}] 
  ▼ 0:
      avatar_url: "https://avatars.githubusercontent.com/u/1658846?v=4"
      events_url: "https://api.github.com/users/greg/events{/privacy}"
      followers_url: "https://api.github.com/users/greg/followers"
      following_url: "https://api.github.com/users/greg/following{/other_user}"
      gists_url: "https://api.github.com/users/greg/gists{/gist_id}"
      gravatar_id: ""
      html_url: "https://github.com/greg"
      id: 1658846
      login: "greg"
      node_id: "MDQ6VXNlcjE2NTg4NDY="
      organizations_url: "https://api.github.com/users/greg/orgs"
      received_events_url: "https://api.github.com/users/greg/received_events"
      repos_url: "https://api.github.com/users/greg/repos"
```

Figure 3

Storing our Results

Now that we have made a successful connection to our API, let's have a data variable to store our results instead of just logging them to the console. This lets us display the results to the user. In GitHub.vue, add in the code in **bold**:

Modify Bold Code

```
<script>
export default{
    data(){
      return {
          users:[]
      }
    },
    methods:{
        async fetchGitHubUsers(){
            const res = await fetch(
                    'https://api.github.com/search/users?q=greg')
            const data = await res.json()
            return data.items
        },
    },
    async created(){
        this.users = await this.fetchGitHubUsers()
    }
}
</script>
```

In *data()*, we declare the data variable *users* and set it to an initial value of an empty array [ ]. A variable in *data* can be set to any type, String, Array, Boolean, Integer, Object etc.

And after *await*, instead of logging to the console, we return and assign the results to *users*.

Implementing a GitHub Results Display Page

We now implement a page to display our GitHub user data nicely like in figure 4.

Id	Avatar	Login	URL
1658846		greg	https://github.com/greg
14953		gregkh	https://github.com/gregkh
4739311		gregsometimes	https://github.com/gregsometimes
234804		greggman	https://github.com/greggman
266302		gregberge	https://github.com/gregberge
19739546		gsurma	https://github.com/gsurma

Figure 4

We will use the Table component in Bootstrap (https://getbootstrap.com/docs/5.2/content/tables/).

In GitHub.vue, we add the markup into our component as shown below:

Modify Bold Code

```
<script>
...
...
...
</script>
<template>
```

```
<table class="table">
  <thead>
    <tr>
      <th scope="col">Id</th>
      <th scope="col">Avatar</th>
      <th scope="col">Login</th>
      <th scope="col">URL</th>
    </tr>
  </thead>
  <tbody>
    <tr :key="user.id" v-for="user in users">
      <th scope="row">{{user.id}}</th>
      <td><img :alt='user.login' :src='user.avatar_url' width="75"
height="75"/></td>
      <td>{{user.login}}</td>
      <td><a :href="user.html_url">{{user.html_url}}</a></td>
    </tr>
  </tbody>
</table>
</template>
```

Code Explanation

We use the *v-for* loop to repeat the table row for each user data we get from GitHub.

We then add JavaScript expressions wrapped in {{}} inside the template ie.: user's id, login, html_url, and avatar_url.

We resize the user picture i.e.: *user.avatar_url* with *width*, *height* attributes. We also create a href link with *user.html_url*. When you click it, you are brought to the user's GitHub page.

* Note that we have to use *v-bind* for attributes:
e.g. :alt='user.login', :src='user.avatar_url', :href="user.html_url"

If you run your app now, you should get a similar page as shown below (fig. 5).

Id	Avatar	Login	URL
1658846		greg	https://github.com/greg
14953		gregkh	https://github.com/gregkh
4739311		gregsometimes	https://github.com/gregsometimes
234804		greggman	https://github.com/greggman
266302		gregberge	https://github.com/gregberge
19739546		gsurma	https://github.com/gsurma

Figure 5

Adding an Input to GitHub Results Display Page

We currently hard-code our search term to *'greg'* in our request to GitHub. Let's create a data variable *searchTerm* so that a user can type in her search terms and retrieve the relevant search results.

Declare and append *searchTerm* to our URL by adding the below codes in **bold**:

Modify Bold Code

```
<script>
export default{
    data(){
      return {
          users:[],
          searchTerm: ''
      }
    },
    methods:{
        async fetchGitHubUsers(){
            const res = await fetch(
            `https://api.github.com/search/users?q=${this.searchTerm}`)

            const data = await res.json()
```

70

```
        return data.items
    },
...
...
...
```

Take note that we change from using double quotes "" to using backticks `` ` ` `` to allow appending the search term in the above manner.

Next, we create a separate function *onSubmit()* that will be called when a user clicks 'Submit' on a search form. Make the following code changes:

Modify Bold Code

```
...
    methods:{
        async fetchGitHubUsers(){
            ...
            ...
            ...
        },
        async onSubmit(e){
            this.users = await this.fetchGitHubUsers()
        }
    },
...
```

Next, add a *Form* with *input* element as shown in **bold**:

Modify Bold Code

```
...
...
...
<template>
<form @submit.prevent="onSubmit">
  <div class="mb-3">
    <input v-model="searchTerm" type="text" class="form-control">
  </div>
  <button type="submit" class="btn btn-primary">Submit</button>
</form>
<table class="table">
...
...
```

When you run your app now, it renders a simple form with a single input (fig. 6) binded to the state's *searchTerm* property.

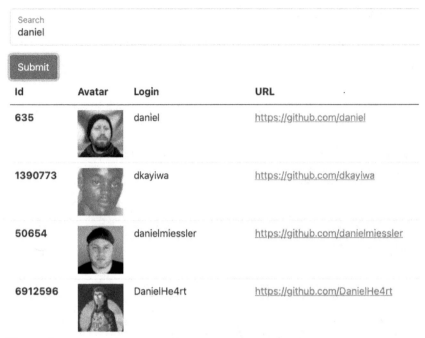

Figure 6

When the user types in a search term and clicks 'Search', you can now see GitHub user results.

Showing a Loader Icon

While getting content from a server, it is often useful to show a loading spinner icon to the user (fig. 7).

figure 7

To do so, in GitHub component, create a data variable called *isLoading* and set it to *true* like in the below code:

Modify Bold Code

```
<script>
export default{
    data(){
        return {
            users:[],
            searchTerm: 'greg',
            isLoading: false
```

```
    }
  },
...
```

isLoading will be true when loading of results from the server is still going on. We set it to false in the beginning.

We set *isLoading* to true before the call to *fetch* in *fetchGitHubUsers* (called when a user submits the form):

Modify Bold Code

```
...
    methods:{
        async fetchGitHubUsers(){
            ...
        },
        async onSubmit(e){
            this.isLoading = true;
            this.users = await this.fetchGitHubUsers()
        }
    },
...
```

Once we are notified of results from the GitHub request, we set *isLoading* to *false* in *getData* to hide the spinner:

Modify Bold Code

```
...
    methods:{
        async fetchGitHubUsers(){
            const res = await fetch(
            `https://api.github.com/search/users?q=${this.searchTerm}`)
            const data = await res.json()
            this.isLoading = false;
            return data.items
        },
...
```

Next in the markup, we render a spinner:

Modify Bold Code

```
<template>
<form @submit.prevent="onSubmit">
  ...
</form>
<div v-if='isLoading' class="spinner-border" role="status">
</div>
<table class="table">
  ...
```

We use the *v-if* conditional to make the *Spinner* visible only when the component is loading. Bootstrap provides many easy to use spinners (https://getbootstrap.com/docs/5.2/components/spinners/ - fig. 8).

Colors

The border spinner uses currentColor for its border-color, utilities. You can use any of our text color utilities on the stand

Figure 8

Running your App

If you load your app in the browser, you should see the Spinner being displayed for a short moment before data from the server is loaded.

You can try out other kinds of spinners as specified in the Bootstrap documentation.

Summary

In the chapter, we learned how to implement a GitHub User Search application by connecting our React app to the GitHub RESTful API using *fetch*, Promises, component lifecycles and displaying a loader icon.

Contact support@i-ducate.com if you have not already had the full source code for this chapter.

CHAPTER 7: TO-DO C.R.U.D. APP

Project Setup for our To-Do C.R.U.D. App

In this chapter, we will create a To-do app to create, read, update, delete and mark-complete to-dos (fig. 1).

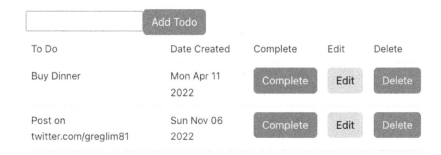

Figure 1

In the next chapter, we will then see how to connect our app to an external API to persist our data. This app will teach you fundamentals on how to build larger and more complicated apps.

First, create a new project with:

Execute in Terminal

```
npm init vue@latest
```

You will be asked some questions.
- For "Project name", enter 'VueTodo'
- For "Add Vue Router for Single Page Application development", enter 'No' (we will illustrate Vue Router later)
- Enter 'No' for the rest.
-

Next, run the following:

```
cd Vuetodo
npm install
```

Fake Data

We will first have some fake data in App.vue to define our initial *to-dos*. Later, we will implement getting data from a REST API.

In App.vue, define our initial *todos* with the following code:

```
<template>
</template>
<script>
export default{
  data(){
    return{
      todos:[]
    }
  },
  created(){
    this.todos = [
      {
        id:1,
        text: "finishing writing Vue book",
        complete: false,
        date: new Date().toDateString(),
        dateCompleted: null
      },
      {
        id:2,
        text: "play with kids",
        complete: false,
        date: new Date().toDateString(),
        dateCompleted: null
      },
      {
        id:3,
        text: "read bible",
        complete: false,
        date: new Date().toDateString(),
        dateCompleted: null
      }
    ]
  }
}
```

```
</script>
```

Code Explanation

We define an array *todos* in *data()*. In *created()*, we assign an array of *todo* objects as the default *todos* state. Remember that we commonly use *created* lifecycle method to make data requests. In a future chapter, we will replace the hard-coding of data with HTTP requests.

ToDoList component

In *src/components*, remove all the folders and files in it. And create a new file *ToDoList.vue* to list our todos with the following code:

Add Code
```
<script>
export default{
    props: {
        todos: Array
    }
}
</script>

<template>
<div>
    <li v-for="todo in todos" :key="todo.id">{{todo.text}}</li>
</div>
</template>
```

Code Explanation

We define a prop *todos* which will be passed in from App.vue's *todos* when it instantiates ToDoList. We then proceed to *loop* and list out the todo items.

Running our App

Back in *App.vue*, import *ToDoList* and render it:

Replace Entire Code
```
<template>
<div>
<ToDoList :todos="todos" />
</div>
</template>
<script>
import ToDoList from './components/ToDoList.vue'
```

```
export default{
  components:{
    ToDoList
  },
  ...
}
</script>
```

Now, run your app with *npm run dev* in the Terminal, and you should see an initial list of *todos* displayed (fig. 2).

- finishing writing Vue book
- play with kids
- read bible

Figure 2

Styling our *ToDoList*

Our list of todos currently looks rather plain. Let's apply some styling from Bootstrap. We will use the *Table* component again to list our todos in a table. (Remember to include the Bootstrap CDN in index.html)

In *src/components/ToDoList.vue*, add the following in **bold**:

```
                    Modify Bold Code
<script>
export default{
    props: {
        todos: Array
    }
}
</script>

<template>
<div>
<table class="table">
  <thead>
    <tr>
      <th scope="col">To Do</th>
      <th scope="col">Date Created</th>
      <th scope="col">Complete</th>
```

```
      <th scope="col">Edit</th>
      <th scope="col">Delete</th>
    </tr>
  </thead>
  <tbody>
    <tr v-for="todo in todos" :key="todo.id">
       <th scope="row">{{todo.text}}</th>
       <td>{{todo.date}}</td>
       <td>Mark Complete</td>
       <td>Edit</td>
       <td>Delete</td>
    </tr>
  </tbody>
</table>
</div>
</template>
```

Our table has five columns, the Todo text, date created, Mark-Complete, *Edit* and *Delete* columns.

When we run our app now, our *todos* should be displayed in a table (fig. 3):

To Do	Date Created	Complete	Edit	Delete
finishing writing Vue book	Mon Oct 31 2022	Mark Complete	Edit	Delete
play with kids	Mon Oct 31 2022	Mark Complete	Edit	Delete
read bible	Mon Oct 31 2022	Mark Complete	Edit	Delete

Figure 3

Removing a Todo

Let's see how to remove (delete) a todo. We want to remove a todo upon clicking on 'Delete'. In the delete *td*, add a Button with its *on:click* handler:

ToDoList.vue

Modify Bold Code
```
<script>
export default{
    props: {
        todos: Array
    },
    emits:['delete-todo']
}
```

```
</script>
<template>
<div>
<table class="table">
  <thead>
    ...
  </thead>
  <tbody>
    <tr v-for="todo in todos" :key="todo.id">
        <th scope="row">{{todo.text}}</th>
        <td>{{todo.date}}</td>
        <td>Mark Complete</td>
        <td>Edit</td>
        <td>
          <button @click="$emit('delete-todo',todo.id)"
            class="btn btn-danger">
            Delete
          </button>
        </td>
    </tr>
  </tbody>
</table>
</div>
</template>
```

@click emits the 'delete-todo' custom event with the built in *$emit* method. This will later be listened by the parent, App.vue.

$emit takes an event name as its first argument, which is what the parent component will listen for. We can also provide additional arguments that will be passed as parameters to any listening callback functions. In our case, we provide *todo.id* to be emitted: `$emit('delete-todo',todo.id)`

*Note: We recommend using kebab-cased event names (eg. 'delete-todo') to avoid any automatic case transformation issues

Because deleting a to-do is a dangerous action, we set its class to 'btn-danger' to have it in red color. Note that we have to declare the 'delete-todo' event in the component via the *emits* option:

```
<script>
export default{
    props: {
        todos: Array
    },
    emits:['delete-todo']
}
</script>
```

We next handle the 'delete-todo' event in *App.vue*:

Modify Bold Code

```
<template>
<div>
<ToDoList :todos="todos" @delete-todo="deleteTodo" />
</div>
</template>
<script>
import ToDoList from './components/ToDoList.vue'

export default{
  components:{
    ToDoList
  },
  data(){
    ...
  },
  methods:{
    deleteTodo(todoId){
      if(confirm('Are you sure?')){
        this.todos = this.todos.filter((todo) => todo.id !== todoId)
      }
    }
  }
  ...
}
</script>
```

Code Explanation

```
<ToDoList :todos="todos" @delete-todo="deleteTodo" />
```

We listen to the 'delete-todo' event in the parent (App.vue) and specify a listener method, *deleteTodo* to handle the event.

In our app, we will channel all the events to App.vue to access its *todos* array. App.vue acts (in some sense) as a data store.

```
  methods:{
    deleteTodo(todoId){
      if(confirm('Are you sure?')){
        this.todos = this.todos.filter((todo) => todo.id !== todoId)
      }
    }
  }
```

We then implement the delete logic in *deleteTodo*. *todos.filter* checks for each element and filters for only *todo* objects whose id is not equal to the id of the todo to be deleted.

If we run our app now, and click on 'Delete' for a todo, that todo will be removed (fig. 4).

To Do	Date Created	Complete	Edit	Delete
finishing writing Vue book	Mon Oct 31 2022	Mark Complete	Edit	Delete
play with kids	Mon Oct 31 2022	Mark Complete	Edit	Delete
read bible	Mon Oct 31 2022	Mark Complete	Edit	Delete

Figure 4

Adding Todos

To let users create a todo, we will have a form on the top of our *ToDoList* component (fig. 5).

To Do	Date Created	Complete	Edit	Delete
Buy Dinner	Mon Apr 11 2022	Mark Complete	Edit	Delete

Figure 5

We went through forms in chapter six. So, we will skip some explanations regarding implementation of a form. In */src/components*, create a file AddTodo.vue and add in the below code:

Add Code

```
<script>
export default{
    data(){
        return{
            text:''
        }
    },
    methods:{
```

```
            onSubmit(e){
                ...
            }
        }
}
</script>
<template>
<form @submit.prevent="onSubmit">
    <input v-model="text" type="text">
    <button type="submit" class="btn btn-primary">Add Todo</button>
</form>
</template>
```

Code Explanation

Analyze Code

```
    data(){
        return{
            text:''
        }
    },
```

We store the user-entered todo text in *text*.

We declare a *onSubmit* (we will add in more details later) and bind it to the Form's *submit* event.

Analyze Code

```
...
    methods:{
        onSubmit(e){
            ...
        }
    }
}
</script>
<template>
<form @submit.prevent="onSubmit">
    <input v-model="text" type="text">
    <button type="submit" class="btn btn-primary">Add Todo</button>
</form>
</template>
```

In our form, we have a form input control for users to enter the todo text. We bind the input control's value to *text*. This should be familiar to you as we have gone through them in the previous chapters.

onSubmit

We then implement *onSubmit* with:

```
                        Modify Bold Code
    ...
    onSubmit(e){
        if(!this.text){
            alert("Please enter todo text");
            return
        }
        else{
            const newTodo = {
                id: Math.floor(Math.random() * 100000),
                text: this.text,
                complete: false,
                date: new Date().toDateString(),
                dateCompleted: false
            }

            this.$emit('add-todo',newTodo)
            this.text = ''
        }
    }
    ...
```

Code Explanation

In *onSubmit*, we first check if *text* has a value (which means that the user has entered into the textfield). If so, we create a *newTodo* object. We generate an id with *Math.floor(Math.random() * 100000)*. This will later be replaced with a truly unique id generator when we connect it with our backend API.

We assign *text* with the user-input text and set the *todo* date to the current date with *new Date()*.

We then emit the 'add-todo' event with *newTodo* as argument.

Handling 'add-todo' event

We next handle the 'add-todo' event in *App.vue*:

Modify Bold Code

```
<template>
<div>
<AddTodo @add-todo="addTodo" />
<ToDoList :todos="todos" @delete-todo="deleteTodo" />
</div>
</template>
<script>
import ToDoList from './components/ToDoList.vue'
import AddTodo from './components/AddTodo.vue'

export default{
  components:{
    ToDoList,
    AddTodo
  },
  data(){
      ...
  },
  methods:{
    deleteTodo(todoId){
        ...
    },
    addTodo(todo){
      this.todos = [...this.todos,todo]
    }
  }
  ...
}
</script>
```

The 'add-todo' event will be handled by *addTodo*, which creates a new array with the existing *todos* ('...' spread operator) and adds *newToDo* to it.

We also import and render the *AddTodo* component on top of the *ToDoList* component in the template.

When we run our app, our TodoForm will appear. If we don't enter a todo text and click the 'Add Todo' button, we will get an alert (fig. 6):

85

localhost:5173
localhost:5173 says
Please enter todo text
OK
Add Todo
To Do
finishing writing Vue book
Fri Oct 14 2022
Mark Complete
play with kids
Fri Oct 14 2022
Mark Complete

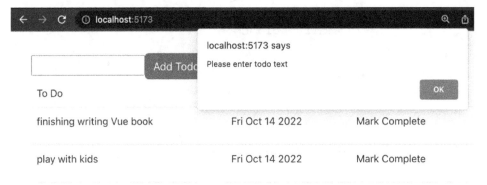

Figure 6

If we enter a todo text, it gets added to the todo list (fig. 7).

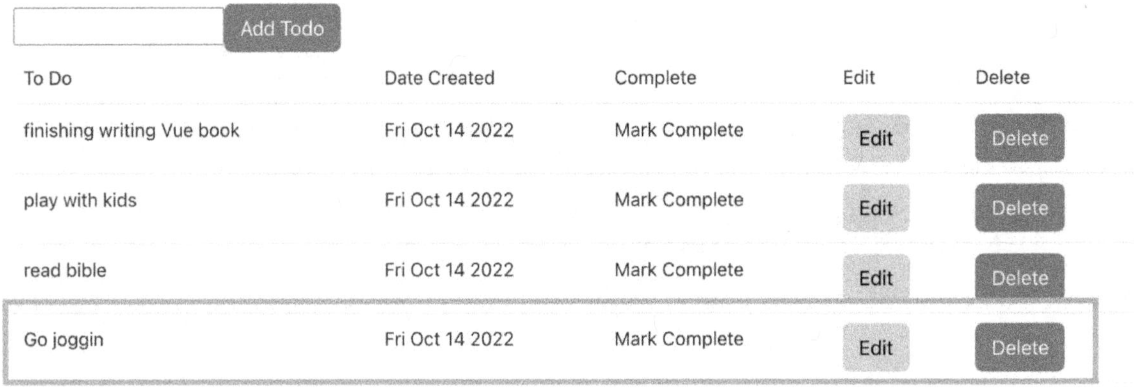

Add Todo
To Do
Date Created
Complete
Edit
Delete
finishing writing Vue book
Fri Oct 14 2022
Mark Complete
Edit
Delete
play with kids
Fri Oct 14 2022
Mark Complete
Edit
Delete
read bible
Fri Oct 14 2022
Mark Complete
Edit
Delete
Go joggin
Fri Oct 14 2022
Mark Complete
Edit
Delete

Figure 7

Editing Todos

Next, we want to implement editing our to-dos. A user will first click on the 'Edit' of the todo row she wishes to edit. That todo text will then appear in the form field for her to edit.

App.vue

To do so, we add an *editMode* and *editTodo* to *App.vue*'s *data()*:

Modify Bold Code

```
...
export default{
  components:{
    ToDoList,
    AddTodo,
    EditTodo
  },
  data(){
    return{
      todos:[],
      editMode: false,
      editTodo: null
    }
  },
...
```

editMode will be set to true when a user clicks on an 'Edit'. *editTodo* will contain the specific todo object to be edited.

Next, we import and render a separate EditTodo component (similar to AddTodo) that when *editMode* is true, will be rendered instead of AddTodo. We pass in *editTodo* into EditTodo as props. When *editMode* is false, we render AddTodo. Modify the below codes in **bold** to implement this:

Modify Bold Code

```
<template>
<div>
<EditTodo v-if="editMode" :editTodo="editTodo" :key="editTodo.id"/>
<AddTodo v-else @add-todo="addTodo" />
<ToDoList :todos="todos" @delete-todo="deleteTodo" />
</div>
</template>

<script>
import ToDoList from './components/ToDoList.vue'
import AddTodo from './components/AddTodo.vue'
import EditTodo from './components/EditTodo.vue'

export default{
  components:{
    ToDoList,
    AddTodo,
    EditTodo
  },
...
...
```

...

Note that we need to include *:key="editTodo.id"* in EditTodo. This is to ensure that EditTodo knows which *editTodo* object to render for editing.

ToDoList.vue

But where do we get *editTodo* from? We will need to get it from ToDoList. Add an Edit button in each row of ToDoList with the below code in **bold**:

Modify Bold Code

```
<script>
export default{
    props: {
        todos: Array
    },
    emits:['delete-todo','edit-todo']
}
</script>

<template>
<div>
<table class="table">
  <thead>
     ...
  </thead>
  <tbody>
    <tr v-for="todo in todos" :key="todo.id">
        <th scope="row">{{todo.text}}</th>
        <td>{{todo.date}}</td>
        <td>Mark Complete</td>
        <td>
          <button @click="$emit('edit-todo',todo)"
            class="btn btn-warning">
            Edit
          </button>
        </td>
        <td>
          <button @click="$emit('delete-todo',todo.id)"
            class="btn btn-danger">
            Delete
          </button>
        </td>
    </tr>
  </tbody>
</table>
```

88

```
</div>
</template>
```

We register the 'edit-todo' event in ToDoList in the *emits* option.

The Edit button emits the custom 'edit-todo' event with the todo to be edited as argument.

Again, we handle the 'edit-todo' event in App.vue (see how App.vue acts as the central place where we handle all 'CRUD' operations?).

In App.vue, add the below codes in **bold**:

Modify Bold Code

```
<template>
<div>
<EditTodo v-if="editMode" :editTodo="editTodo" :key="editTodo.id"/>
<AddTodo v-else @add-todo="addTodo" />
<ToDoList :todos="todos" @delete-todo="deleteTodo"
@edit-todo="handleEdit"/>
</div>
</template>

<script>
...

export default{
  components:{
      ...
  },
  data(){
      ...
  },
  methods:{
    deleteTodo(todoId){
      ...
    },
    addTodo(todo){
      ...
    },
    handleEdit(todo){
      this.editMode = true
      this.editTodo = todo
    },
...
...
...
```

Code Explanation

```
<ToDoList :todos="todos" @delete-todo="deleteTodo"
@edit-todo="handleEdit"/>
```

We specify that ToDoList will trigger a custom event 'edit-todo' and call the function *handleEdit*. We then define *handleEdit* as:

```
methods:{
  deleteTodo(todoId){
    ...
  },
  addTodo(todo){
    ...
  },
  handleEdit(todo){
    this.editMode = true
    this.editTodo = todo
  },
```

handleEdit sets *editMode* to true and provide us with the todo to be edited (passed in from TodoList).

We then pass *editTodo* into ToDoEditForm:

Analyze Code
```
<template>
<EditTodo v-if="editMode" :editTodo="editTodo" :key="editTodo.id"/>

...
```

EditTodo

Let's now create the EditTodo component. EditTodo will be quite similar to AddTodo. We can in fact combine them, but for simplicity's sake in learning, we create a separate form.

In *components*, create a new file EditTodo.vue and copy paste the codes from AddTodo.vue into it.

Make the following additions:

Modify Bold Code
```
<script>
export default{
    props: {
        editTodo: null
    },
```

```
    data(){
        return{
            text:''
        }
    },
    methods:{
        onSubmit(e){
            ...
        }
    },
    created(){
        this.text = this.editTodo.text
    },
}

</script>
<template>
<form @submit.prevent="onSubmit">
    <input v-model="text" type="text">
    <button type="submit" class="btn btn-primary">Edit Todo</button>
</form>
</template>
```

We create the *editTodo* prop to receive it from App.vue. We use *editTodo* to populate our Edit Form in the *created* lifecycle method. We also change the label for the button to 'Edit Todo'.

With this, we populate the form's field with the todo's text to be edited.

Testing our App

Now let's test our app to see if we can populate the Edit form when we click on a particular todo.

When you run your app and click on a to-do, the text appears in the form's field for you to edit (fig. 8).

To Do	Date Created	Complete	Edit	Delete
finishing writing Vue book	Fri Oct 14 2022	Mark Complete	Edit	Delete
play with kids	Fri Oct 14 2022	Mark Complete	Edit	Delete
read bible	Fri Oct 14 2022	Mark Complete	Edit	Delete

Figure 8

Notice that the button's text also changes to 'Edit Todo' since we are displaying EditTodo instead of AddTodo now.

onSubmit

Now that we have populated the Edit Form, let's implement the actual editing of the todo.

In EditTodo.vue, implement *onSubmit* as:

```
                          Modify Bold Code
<script>
export default{
    ...
    methods:{
        onSubmit(e){
            if(!this.text){
                alert("Please enter todo text");
                return
            }
            else{
                const editedTodo = {
                    ...this.editTodo,
                    text: this.text,
                }

                this.$emit('submit-edit',editedTodo)
                this.text = ''
            }
        }
    },
    created(){
        ...
    },
    emits:['submit-edit']
}
...
```

onSubmit is similar to the one in AddTodo.vue, except that we create an *editedTodo* instance with the updated text. We then emit the custom event 'submit-edit' with *editedTodo* as argument.

We have to specify with the *emits* option that we are emitting the 'submit-edit' event.

We next handle the event in App.vue. In *App.vue*, we create a new method *submitEdit* by modifying the codes in **bold**:

Modify Bold Code

```
<template>
<div>
<EditTodo v-if="editMode" :editTodo="editTodo" @submit-
edit="submitEdit" :key="editTodo.id"/>
<AddTodo v-else @add-todo="addTodo" />
<ToDoList :todos="todos" @delete-todo="deleteTodo" @edit-
todo="handleEdit"/>
</div>
</template>

...
  methods:{
    deleteTodo(todoId){

      ...
    },
    addTodo(todo){

      ...
    },
    handleEdit(todo){

      ...
    },
    submitEdit(editedTodo){
      this.todos = this.todos.map(
        (todo) => todo.id === editedTodo.id ?
            {...todo, text: editedTodo.text} : todo
      )
      this.editMode = false
      this.editTodo = null
    }
  },
...
```

Code Explanation

```
<template>
<EditTodo v-if="editMode" :editTodo="editTodo" @submit-
edit="submitEdit" :key="editTodo.id"/>
```

We specify that the *submitEdit* method handles the 'submit-edit' event.

```
    submitEdit(editedTodo){
      this.todos = this.todos.map(
        (todo) => todo.id === editedTodo.id ?
            {...todo, text: editedTodo.text} : todo
      )
      this.editMode = false
```

93

```
    this.editTodo = null
  }
```

submitEdit receives *editedToDo* (which contains the updated todo text) from EditTodo component. Next, using *map()*, we create a new array by checking on every element in the array. If its id is the edited todo's id, replace the text with the updated todo text. Else, just return the original todo object.

When that's done, we set *editMode* to false (since editing is completed) so that our app displays the AddTodo form by default.

Running our App

When we run our app now, we can select a todo and then update its text.

Summary

Congratulations if you made it thus far! In the next chapter, we will see how to persist our data by connecting to an external API.

And in case you are lost, below's the full source code.

App.vue

```
<template>
<div>
<EditTodo v-if="editMode" :editTodo="editTodo" @submit-
edit="submitEdit" :key="editTodo.id"/>
<AddTodo v-else @add-todo="addTodo" />
<ToDoList :todos="todos" @delete-todo="deleteTodo" @edit-
todo="handleEdit"/>
</div>
</template>
<script>
import ToDoList from './components/ToDoList.vue'
import AddTodo from './components/AddTodo.vue'
import EditTodo from './components/EditTodo.vue'

export default{
  components:{
    ToDoList,
    AddTodo,
    EditTodo
  },
  data(){
    return{
```

```
      todos:[],
          editMode: false,
          editTodo: null
    }
  },
  methods:{
    deleteTodo(todoId){
      if(confirm('Are you sure?')){
        this.todos = this.todos.filter((todo) => todo.id !== todoId)
      }
    },
    addTodo(todo){
      this.todos = [...this.todos,todo]
    },
    handleEdit(todo){
      this.editMode = true
      this.editTodo = todo
    },
    submitEdit(editedTodo){
      this.todos = this.todos.map(
        (todo) => todo.id === editedTodo.id ?
          {...todo, text: editedTodo.text} : todo
      )
      this.editMode = false
      this.editTodo = null
    }

  },
  created(){
    this.todos = [
      {
        id:1,
        text: "finishing writing Vue book",
        complete: false,
        date: new Date().toDateString(),
        dateCompleted: null
      },
      {
        id:2,
        text: "play with kids",
        complete: false,
        date: new Date().toDateString(),
        dateCompleted: null
      },
      {
        id:3,
        text: "read bible",
        complete: false,
```

```
            date: new Date().toDateString(),
            dateCompleted: null
        }
    ]
  }
}
</script>
```

ToDoList.vue

Analyze Code

```
<script>
export default{
    props: {
        todos: Array
    },
    emits:['delete-todo','edit-todo']
}
</script>

<template>
<div>
<table class="table">
  <thead>
    <tr>
      <th scope="col">To Do</th>
      <th scope="col">Date Created</th>
      <th scope="col">Complete</th>
      <th scope="col">Edit</th>
      <th scope="col">Delete</th>
    </tr>
  </thead>
  <tbody>
    <tr v-for="todo in todos" :key="todo.id">
        <th scope="row">{{todo.text}}</th>
        <td>{{todo.date}}</td>
        <td>Mark Complete</td>
        <td>
          <button @click="$emit('edit-todo',todo)"
            class="btn btn-warning">
            Edit
          </button>
        </td>
        <td>
          <button @click="$emit('delete-todo',todo.id)"
            class="btn btn-danger">
            Delete
```

```
            </button>
        </td>
    </tr>
  </tbody>
</table>
</div>
</template>
```

AddTodo.vue

Analyze Code

```
<script>
export default{
    data(){
        return{
            text:''
        }
    },
    methods:{
        onSubmit(e){
            if(!this.text){
                alert("Please enter todo text");
                return
            }
            else{
                const newTodo = {
                    id: Math.floor(Math.random() * 100000),
                    text: this.text,
                    complete: false,
                    date: new Date().toDateString(),
                    dateCompleted: false
                }

                this.$emit('add-todo',newTodo)
                this.text = ''
            }

        }
    }
}
</script>
<template>
<form @submit.prevent="onSubmit">
    <input v-model="text" type="text">
    <button type="submit" class="btn btn-primary">Add Todo</button>
</form>
</template>
```

EditTodo.vue

Analyze Code

```
<script>
export default{
    props: {
        editTodo: null
    },
    data(){
        return{
            text:''
        }
    },
    methods:{
        onSubmit(e){
            if(!this.text){
                alert("Please enter todo text");
                return
            }
            else{
                const editedTodo = {
                    ...this.editTodo,
                    text: this.text,
                }

                this.$emit('submit-edit',editedTodo)
                this.text = ''
            }
        }
    },
    created(){
        this.text = this.editTodo.text
    },
    emits:['submit-edit']
}
</script>
<template>
<form @submit.prevent="onSubmit">
    <input v-model="text" type="text">
    <button type="submit" class="btn btn-primary">Edit Todo</button>
</form>
</template>
```

CHAPTER 8: CONNECTING TO AN API TO PERSIST DATA

We have made progress in our To-do app. But our data is not yet persistent. When we reload our application, all the changes we have done to our data are gone. In this chapter, we will connect to an API to enable persistency in create, read, update and delete todos.

The API we are connecting to can be supported by any backend, e.g. Nodejs, Firebase, ASP.Net etc. Setting up a backend is obviously beyond the scope of this book. But to quickly set up a mock API, we will use *json-server* (*github.com/typicode/json-server*) which makes it easy to set up JSON APIs for use in demos and proof of concepts.

In a new Terminal, go to the folder containing your Vue projects and run:

Execute in Terminal

```
npm install -g json-server
```

(Note: you might need *sudo*)

Next, create a new folder called *backendapp* and prepare a *todos.json* file which contains the following:

Add Code

```
{
  "todos": [
    {
      "id": "1",
      "text": "Fetch Kid from Tuition",
      "complete": false,
      "date": "Mon Apr 11 2022",
      "dateCompleted": false
    },
    {
      "id": "2",
      "text": "Buy Dinner",
      "complete": false,
      "date": "Mon Apr 11 2022",
      "dateCompleted": false
    },
    {
      "id": "3",
      "text": "Post on twitter.com/greglim81",
      "complete": false,
      "date": "Mon Apr 11 2022",
```

```
      "dateCompleted": false
    }
  ]
}
```

These are similar to the *todos* we have in App.vue.

Back in Terminal, in the folder that contains *todos.json*, run the command:

```
json-server -p 4000 todos.json
```

This will run a mock REST API server in your local machine and you can see the endpoint at:

```
http://localhost:4000/todos
```

The endpoint will return an array of *todos* just like back in App.vue.

Now that we have a mock REST API running, let's connect to it from our Vue app. You can imagine that the REST API is deployed on a server in a real-world scenario. Simply change the URL of the endpoint to point to the server. The rest of the code remains the same.

Using *created* to Fetch Initial App Data

Because we are retrieving our to-dos from the API, our initial *todos* in *App.vue* (in the *VueToDo* project) will just be an empty array.

```
...
export default{
      ...
  created(){
    this.todos = []
  }
}
</script>
```

We will instead call our API to populate *todos*. In App.vue, add the following code in **bold**:

```
...
<script>
import ToDoList from './components/ToDoList.vue'
...'

export default{
```

```
  components:{
     ...
  },
  data(){
    return{
      todos:[],
      editMode: false,
      editTodo: null,
      endpoint: "http://localhost:4000/todos/"
    }
  },
  methods:{
     ...
    submitEdit(editedTodo){
       ...
    },
    async fetchTodos(){
      const res = await fetch(this.endpoint)
      const data = await res.json()
      return data
    }
  },
  async created(){
    this.todos = await this.fetchTodos()
  }
}
</script>
```

We created a new method *fetchTodos*. In it, we use *fetch* with the endpoint to retrieve data from the API and return the results. Because we use *await* on *fetch*, we need to specify *async* at the declaration.

We use *created* to retrieve data from the endpoint when the component is created.

When we run our app now, we retrieve our todos from the API and display them.

Delete Request to Remove Todos

To delete a todo, we need to get the specific URL for a todo item. We get that by appending the *todo.id* to the endpoint: *endpoint + todo.id*, e.g. *http://localhost:4000/todos/1*

Thus in *App.vue*, in *deleteTodo*, we specify the todo URL, *endpoint + todo.id* to *fetch* to remove the todo with the codes in **bold**:

Modify Bold Code

```
<script>
...
  methods:{
    async deleteTodo(todoId){
      if(confirm('Are you sure?')){
        const res = await fetch(this.endpoint + todoId,{
          method: 'DELETE'
        })
        res.status === 200
          ? (this.todos = this.todos.filter((todo) => todo.id !==
todoId))
          : alert('Error deleting todo')
      }
    },
...
```

Because we use *await* on *fetch*, we need to specify *async* at the declaration of the function.

Run your app now and when you delete a todo, it will be removed.

Performing Post Request to Add Todos

Next, we will perform a post request to add a todo. In *App.vue*, add the following codes in **bold**:

Modify Bold Code

```
...
  methods:{
    async deleteTodo(todoId){
      ...
    },
    async addTodo(todo){
      const res = await fetch(this.endpoint,{
          method: 'POST',
          headers:{
            'Content-type': 'application/json'
          },
          body: JSON.stringify(todo)
        })
      const data = await res.json()
      this.todos = [...this.todos,data]
    },
...
```

Code Explanation

fetch requires two parameters. The first parameter is the URL of the service endpoint. The second parameter is the object which contains the properties we want to send to our server.

We thus call *fetch* with our endpoint and the new todo object. Because we use *await*, we have to label *addTodo* as an asynchronous function with the *async* keyword.

Run your app and you should be able to add todos.

Note that when we add an object into the JSON server, it will automatically assign an id for us (as with most backends). So we can remove assigning of the id in AddTodo.vue:

```
methods:{
    onSubmit(e){
        ...
            const newTodo = {
                //id: Math.floor(Math.random() * 100000),
                text: this.text,
                complete: false,
                date: new Date().toDateString(),
                dateCompleted: false
        }
        ...
```

Performing Patch Request to Update Todos

Finally, let's implement editing a todo. In App.vue, add a few lines of code to *submitEdit*.

Modify Bold Code

```
...
    async submitEdit(editedTodo){
      const res = await fetch(this.endpoint + editedTodo.id,{
          method: 'PUT',
          headers:{
            'Content-type': 'application/json'
          },
          body: JSON.stringify(editedTodo)
      })
      const data = await res.json()

      this.todos = this.todos.map(
        (todo) => todo.id === editedTodo.id
            ? {...todo, text: data.text}
            : todo
```

```
    )
    this.editMode = false
    this.editTodo = null
  },
...
```

We call *fetch* with the specific todo's endpoint and provide the new values to be updated. The rest of the code remains the same. And when we run our app now, we can edit a todo!

In case you got lost in any of the steps, get the full code by contacting support@i-ducate.com.

CHAPTER 9: MARKING TODOS COMPLETE

Let's implement the mark 'Complete' button for each Todo in *ToDoList.vue* (fig. 1).

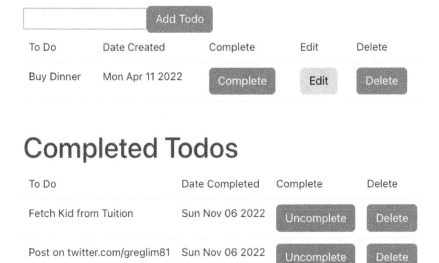

Figure 1

In ToDoList.vue, add the below in **bold**:

```
                    Modify Bold Code
  ...
<tbody>
  <tr v-for="todo in todos" :key="todo.id">
    <template v-if="!todo.complete">
      <th scope="row">{{todo.text}}</th>
      <td>{{todo.date}}</td>
      <td>
        <button @click="$emit('toggle-complete',todo)"
          class="btn btn-success">
          Complete
        </button>
      </td>
      <td>
        <button ...>Edit</button>
      </td>
      <td>
```

```
            <button ...>Delete</button>
          </td>
        </template>
      </tr>
    </tbody>
    ...
```

Wrapping each row in a *<template>* and using *v-if*, we list only uncompleted todos. We will show the completed todos in another section.

We emit the 'toggle-complete' event and pass in the todo when the user clicks on the 'Complete' button. So, let's add 'toggle-complete' to the *emits* option in *<script>*:

```
<script>
export default{
    props: {
        todos: Array
    },
    emits:['delete-todo','edit-todo','toggle-complete']
}
</script>
```

App.vue

Next in App.vue, we handle the 'toggle-complete' event with the code in **bold**:

```
<template>
<div>
<EditTodo .../>
<AddTodo .../>
<ToDoList :todos="todos" @delete-todo="deleteTodo" @edit-todo="handleEdit"
@toggle-complete="toggleComplete"/>
</div>
</template>
```

Next, add in the codes for *toggleComplete* in *methods*:

Modify Bold Code

```
...
  methods:{
    async deleteTodo(todoId){

      ...
    },
    async addTodo(todo){
```

106

```
    …
  },
  handleEdit(todo){

    …
  },
  async submitEdit(editedTodo){

    …
  },
  async fetchTodos(){

    …
  },
  async toggleComplete(todo){

    todo.complete = !todo.complete
    todo.dateCompleted = new Date().toDateString()

    const res = await fetch(this.endpoint + todo.id,{
        method: 'PUT',
        headers:{
          'Content-type': 'application/json'
        },
        body: JSON.stringify(todo)
    })
    const data = await res.json()

    this.todos = this.todos.map(
      (temptodo) => temptodo.id === todo.id
          ? {...temptodo,
              complete: data.complete,
              dateCompleted: data.dateCompleted}
          : temptodo
    )
  },
},
…
```

Code Explanation

toggleComplete is very similar to updating a todo except that it just toggles the todo's *complete* property from false to true (to indicate completion) and vice-versa. We also set *dateCompleted* to the current date.

Rendering a Completed Todo

Currently, completed todos are no longer shown in the todo list. We want to render completed todos in a separate section (fig. 1).

Figure 1

This is pretty straightforward as the code will be similar to how we list todos. To do so, add the below markup into *ToDoList.vue*:

Modify Bold Code

```
...
...
...

<table class="table">
  ...
</table>

<br>
<h1>Completed Todos</h1>

<table class="table">
  <thead>
    <tr>
      <th scope="col">To Do</th>
      <th scope="col">Date Completed</th>
      <th scope="col">Complete</th>
      <th scope="col">Delete</th>
    </tr>
  </thead>
```

```
<tbody>
  <tr v-for="todo in todos" :key="todo.id">
    <template v-if="todo.complete">
      <th scope="row">{{todo.text}}</th>
      <td>{{todo.dateCompleted}}</td>
      <td>
        <button @click="$emit('toggle-complete',todo)"
          class="btn btn-success">
          Uncomplete
        </button>
      </td>
      <td>
        <button @click="$emit('delete-todo',todo.id)"
          class="btn btn-danger">
          Delete
        </button>
      </td>
    </template>
  </tr>
</tbody>
</table>
</div>
</template>
```

The added codes are similar to how we list todos, except that we now show todos only if *todo.complete* is true. For completed todos, we no longer show an edit button (completed todos shouldn't be edited). We continue to show the delete button (for users to remove them) and also the 'Uncomplete' button (in case user has to work on the todo again).

CHAPTER 10: FINAL TOUCHES

This will be a short chapter to illustrate other Vue concepts to put final touches to our application.

Vue Computed Properties

Often, some parts of the component's state need to be computed from other variables and recomputed when they change. For example, we want to display the number of total todos, pending todos, and completed todos (fig. 1).

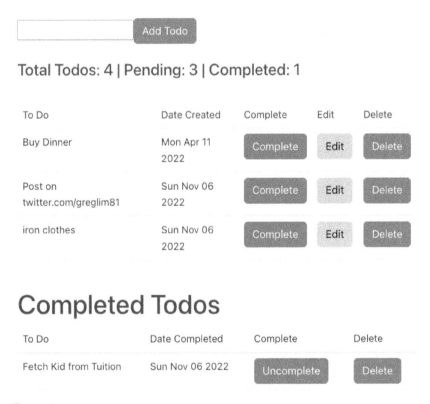

Figure 1

When a user marks a pending todo as complete, the numbers should be recomputed. For these, we use computed properties.

In App.vue, add the following in **bold**:

Modify Bold Code

```
<template>
<div>
<EditTodo …"/>
<AddTodo …/>
<br />
<h4>Total Todos: {{totalTodos}} | Pending: {{pendingTodos}} | Completed:
{{completedTodos}}</h4>
<br />
<ToDoList …/>
</div>
</template>
<script>
…

export default{
  components:{
      …
  },
  data(){
      …
  },
  computed:{
    totalTodos(){
      return this.todos.length
    },
    pendingTodos(){
      return this.todos.filter(
                  todo => {return !todo.complete}
            ).length;
    },
    completedTodos(){
      return this.todos.filter(
                  todo => {return todo.complete}
            ).length;
    }
  },
  methods:{
      …
      …
      …
</script>
```

When we try to make changes to the number of todos (either deleting them or marking them complete/incomplete), **totalTodos, pendingTodos and completedTodos will change accordingly.**

We can data-bind to computed properties in templates just like normal properties. Vue knows that *totalTodos* depends on *this.todos*, so it will update any bindings that depend on *this.totalTodos* when *this.todos* changes.

totalTodos contains the total number of todos in the store.

pendingTodos using the *filter* function, contains only todos that are not completed.

In a similar fashion, *completedTodos* contains only todos that are completed.

When any variable referenced into *totalTodos*, *pendingTodosCount* or *completedTodosCount* changes, Vue will re-run the computation and update the DOM. That is, as you mark todos 'complete' or 'un-complete', Vue re-computes the variables and updates the UI.

Computed Caching vs Methods

You can achieve the same result by instead of having a computed property, define the same function as a method:

```
<h4>Total Todos: {{totalTodos()}} …</h4>

…
  methods:{
    totalTodos(){
      return this.todos.length
    },
…
```

Both will give you the same result. However, computed properties are cached based on their reactive dependencies. A computed property will only re-compute when some of its reactive dependencies have changed. That is, if *todos* have not changed, multiple access to *totalTodos* will immediately return the previously computed result without having the re-compute the function again.

In contrast, a method invocation will always run the function when a re-render occurs. Thus, caching avoids unnecessary expensive re-computation (especially if we have a huge array doing a lot of computations)

However, in cases where you do not want caching, use a method call instead.

Note also that computed functions should only perform pure computation. E.g., don't make async requests to mutate the DOM in a computed function. Computed functions should just return a read-only computed value based on other values.

Vue Router

Let's add a navigation banner to our app so that we can navigate to multiple pages. In our app, we will keep it simple and just have a link to a Home page and an About page. We will display the Todo app in the Home page.

So, create two new files Home.vue and About.vue in /src (same level as App.vue).

About.vue will be a simple view page with the following:

```
<template>
    <h3>About Page</h3>
</template>
```

Move all the codes in App.vue to Home.vue so that App.vue can be the page that contains the router links.

Fill in the following codes into App.vue:

```
<template>
<ul class="nav">
  <li class="nav-item">
    <router-link class="nav-link active" to="/">Home</router-link>
  </li>
  <li class="nav-item">
    <router-link class="nav-link" to="/about">About</router-link>
  </li>
</ul>
<router-view />
</template>
<script>
export default{
}
</script>
```

Code Explanation

The router links are specified using the *<router-link>* tag.

Vue Router provides the *<router-view>* tag to specify where we want the component for each route displayed when that route is active.

/router/index.js

We first install Vue-Router by running in the Terminal:

```
npm install vue-router@4
```

Next in */src*, create a folder */router* and create a file *index.js*. In it, we define our routes to map URLs to components by adding the following code:

```
import { createRouter, createWebHistory } from 'vue-router'
import Home from '../Home.vue'
import About from '../About.vue'

const router = createRouter({
  history: createWebHistory(import.meta.env.BASE_URL),
  routes: [
    {
      path: '/',
      name: 'home',
      component: Home
    },
    {
      path: '/about',
      name: 'about',
      component: About
    }
  ]
})

export default router
```

Code Explanation

We import the *createRouter()* and *createWebHistory()* methods from the Vue Router package.

We call *createRouter()* to create a router instance and pass in a configuration object. There are many configuration options in the object, but we mainly need to specify a *routes* array and a history implementation (we create it with *createWebHistory()*).

The *routes* array defines the URLs you want your app to respond to, and the components they map to.

```
  routes: [
    {
      path: '/',
      name: 'home',
```

```
      component: Home
    },
    {
      path: '/about',
      name: 'about',
      component: About
    }
```

In routes, we have an array of route configuration objects. In each object, we supply a path (i.e. URL) and the component to route to. For example, *Home* component will be rendered when the user navigates to the root URL '/'. *About* component will be rendered when user navigates to '/about'.

main.js

Lastly, in main.js, we configure our app to use the router with the code:

```
import { createApp } from 'vue'
import App from './App.vue'
import router from './router'
import './assets/main.css'

const app = createApp(App)

app.use(router)
app.mount('#app')
```

Running your App

And when you run your app, you can navigate between Home and About pages

Clicking on 'Home' (fig. 2).

Home   About

Total Todos: 5 | Pending: 2 | Completed: 3

To Do	Date Created	Complete	Edit	Delete
Eat lunch	Mon Oct 17 2022	Complete	Edit	Delete
Call Mum	Mon Oct 17 2022	Complete	Edit	Delete

Figure 2

116

Clicking on 'About' (fig. 3).

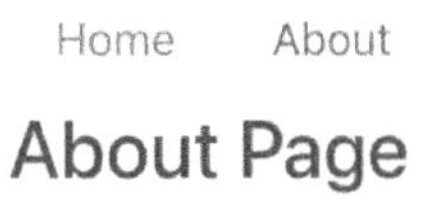

Home   About

About Page

Figure 3

Deployment

In this section, we will deploy our Vue frontend to the Internet to share it with the world. We are going to use Vercel (vercel.com – fig. 4) for our deployment.

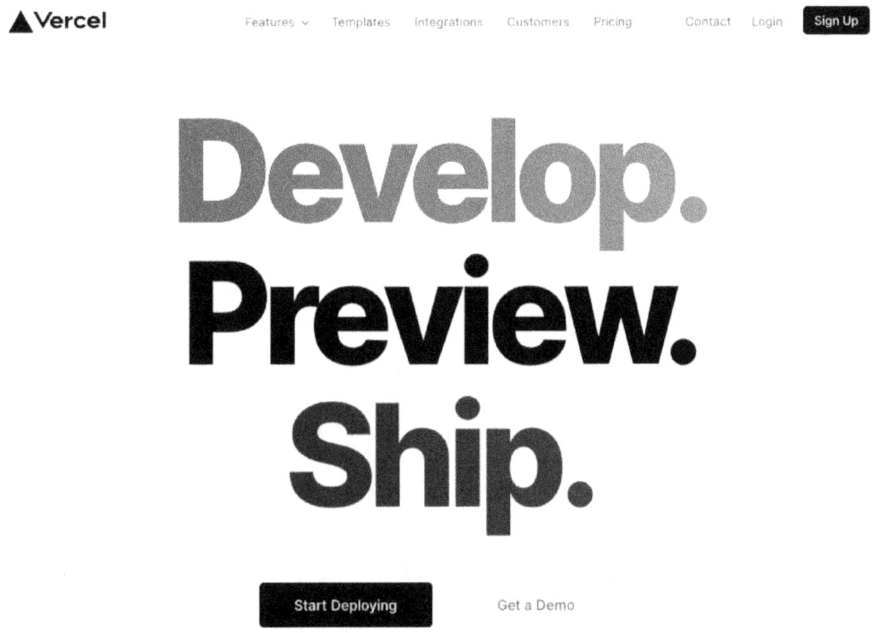

Figure 4

Note: Before deploying on Vercel, you have to replace the fake API URL (e.g. localhost:4000/todos) in your Vue project with the actual live API URL. Do this for all the API calls.

Deploying in Vercel is quite straightforward. You can follow the instructions at: https://vercel.com/guides/deploying-vuejs-to-vercel

We will deploy using the Vercel CLI.

First, in your *VueTodo* project folder, run:

Execute in Terminal

```
npm run build
```

This will create a build version of your app that we can deploy on the web. When the build is finished, you will see a */dist* folder which is what we will deploy.

Next, install the Vercel CLI by running in the Terminal:

Execute in Terminal

```
npm i -g vercel
```

Then, run 'vercel' to deploy. It will prompt you to log in with a Vercel account or sign up if you don't have one.

Answer the questions Vercel prompts you. Vercel will detect you are using Vue, enable the correct settings for your deployment and generate a URL where you can access the page (fig. 5).

```
MacBook-Air-2:VueTodo user$ vercel
Vercel CLI 28.4.11
? Set up and deploy "~/Documents/Vue/VueTodo"? [Y/n] y
? Which scope do you want to deploy to? greglim81
? Link to existing project? [y/N] n
? What's your project's name? vue-todo
? In which directory is your code located? ./
Local settings detected in vercel.json:
Auto-detected Project Settings (Vite):
- Build Command: vite build
- Development Command: vite --port $PORT
- Install Command: `yarn install`, `pnpm install`, or `npm install`
- Output Directory: dist
? Want to modify these settings? [y/N] n
   Linked to greglim81/vue-todo (created .vercel and added it to .gitignore)
   Inspect: https://vercel.com/greglim81/vue-todo/EDdCsuZRnj9U2iw3evrxSmzyV9pF [2s]
   Production: https://vue-todo-rouge.vercel.app [17s]
   Deployed to production. Run `vercel --prod` to overwrite later (https://vercel.link/2F).
   To change the domain or build command, go to https://vercel.com/greglim81/vue-todo/settings
```

Figure 5

Congratulations! Your application is deployed, meaning that your fully functioning Vue app is live and running.

Summary

With this knowledge, you can move on and build more complicated enterprise-level fully functional Vue applications of your own!

Hopefully, you have enjoyed this book and would like to learn more from me. I would love to get your feedback, learning what you liked and didn't for us to improve.

Please feel free to email me at support@i-ducate.com if you encounter any errors with your code, to get updated versions of this book or get the full source code.

If you didn't like the book, or if you feel that I should have covered certain additional topics, please email us to let us know. This book can only get better thanks to readers like you.

Thank you and all the best for your learning journey in Vue!

About the Author

Greg Lim is a technologist and author of several best-selling programming books. Greg has many years in teaching programming in tertiary institutions and he places special emphasis on learning by doing.

Contact Greg at support@i-ducate.com or on Twitter at @greglim81

www.ingramcontent.com/pod-product-compliance
Lightning Source LLC
LaVergne TN
LVHW081530050326
832903LV00025B/1719